# Healthy
# Southwestern
# Cooking

# Healthy Southwestern Cooking

*by* BOB WISEMAN

*photographs by* OWEN LOWE

Northland Publishing

www.northlandpub.com

Tableware and accessories provided courtesy of Dillard's Department Store,
the Kitchen Source, and High Country Style, Flagstaff, Arizona.
Nutritional analysis courtesy of Nutritional Analysis Consultants,
Livonia, Michigan.

Composed in the United States of America
Manufactured in Hong Kong

FIRST IMPRESSION, 1995

05    04    03    02    01      9   8   7   6   5

ISBN 0-87358-618-2

Library of Congress Catalog Card Number Pending

Pictured on the cover: Pequito Tunas Triangles, p. 12.
Pictured on the title page: Chicken Enchiladas, p. 86.
Pictured on the back cover: Grilled Chicken and Zucchini Salad, p. 24.

This book is dedicated to the memory of Bob and Marian Oliver of Silver City, New Mexico. The Olivers taught me about the varieties of chiles and how they are used in southwestern food preparation. I'm sorry that Bob and Marian passed on; they would have enjoyed working with me on this book.

And to Pat Noakes, a tall Texan who stopped in Santa Fe long enough to learn how to cook southwestern fare. I'm glad he spent some time in Las Vegas, Nevada, and shared his cooking skills. Thanks to Pat I learned the Santa Fe way to prepare stacked enchiladas and chile-stuffed filet mignon.

—B. W.

To my wife, Ellen, whose love and support in this oftentimes crazy business is invaluable.

—O. L.

# Contents

A Note from a Registered Dietitian ❖ viii

Introduction ❖ x

Appetizers ❖ 3

Salads ❖ 16

Soups and Stews ❖ 28

Sauces, Stocks, and Basics ❖ 40

Side Dishes ❖ 64

Entrées ❖ 82

Breads, Masa, and Pasta ❖ 130

Desserts ❖ 144

Mail-Order Sources ❖ 151

Acknowledgments ❖ 152

Index ❖ 153

# A Note from a Registered Dietitian

❖

THERE IS A GREAT deal of awareness today about healthy eating, and consumers appreciate having nutritional information so they can make informed decisions about the foods they eat. With this in mind, I founded a business last year to assist food manufacturers, restaurant owners, cookbook authors, hospitals, etc. in providing accurate nutritional analyses of their recipes to their customers. Using my experience as a registered dietitian and my advanced education in dietetics, food service, and nutrition, I work to help the food service industry provide more heart-healthy menus.

I was pleased when I was asked to be an independent consultant to Northland Publishing for *Healthy Southwestern Cooking*. The Center for Science in the Public Interest (a consumer watchdog group that had previously revealed the unhealthy content of Chinese food, Italian meals, and movie theater snacks) had recently released a report on the high-fat, high-salt content of Mexican-style food, and public awareness of the health risks of a diet high in fat and cholesterol was at an all-time high. The book was extremely timely, and I was proud to play a role in the project.

Bob Wiseman, author of *Healthy Southwestern Cooking*, calculated the nutritional facts for the recipes as he composed them. He chose to include the facts that pertain to individuals trying to lower the fat and salt content of their diets: total calories (listed in kilocalories), cholesterol and sodium (in milligrams), and fat and saturated fat (in grams) per serving, as well as the percentage of calories attained from fat. The American Dietetic Association and the American Heart Association recommend that no more than 30 percent of the calories we consume come

❖

from fat, and that no more than 10 percent of the calories should come from saturated fat. In addition, these associations recommend that we consume a diet low in cholesterol (less than 300 milligrams per day) and low in salt.

When I received the *Healthy Southwestern Cooking* manuscript, I was pleased to see the care that Mr. Wiseman had taken in reducing the total fat, cholesterol, and sodium in many of his recipes. I simply went through and—separately from Mr. Wiseman's calculations—figured the nutritional content of each recipe. I adjusted his numbers when necessary. Readers can be assured, then, that each recipe included herein has been analyzed and re-analyzed for accuracy.

Additionally, I have indicated those recipes that meet the American Heart Association's guidelines for heart-healthy eating. Recipes that contain 30 percent or less fat, 10 percent or less saturated fat, and 100 milligrams or less cholesterol are marked with a heart next to the recipe title.

You can live a longer, healthier, and more energetic life by lowering the amount of fat, cholesterol, and sodium in your diet. I hope that the following recipes, with their nutritional information charts, help make this possible for readers and preparers of *Healthy Southwestern Cooking.*

—STEPHEN J. SAPIENZA, M.A., R.D.
*President, Nutritional Analysis Consultants*

# Introduction

ALTHOUGH IT HAS BEEN forty years since I began cooking seriously—and between then and now I have won awards in countless chili contests, attended and taught numerous cooking classes, and had over a hundred recipes published in magazines and newspapers—it took a trip to a doctor to inspire this cookbook.

When the results came back from a blood test and the other tests Doc Forsyth had taken on my body, I was given a lecture, a box of blood pressure pills, and a sheet of paper detailing a bland, boring diet. Then the doctor summarized my treatment: "Less salt. Less fat." Within a few days I regimented to the pills. No hassle there—the little red beasts didn't make me upchuck, get dizzy, or act loco. But the diet, that was another horse.

I couldn't see giving up cooking southwestern vittles. For a day or two I was a confused, hungry man. Then I unsaddled my pride and went to my kitchen, the place where I feel most at home and at ease. It was while assembling a gazpacho that I made a simple discovery: By using a salt substitute and canola oil, I could decrease the fat and sodium intake but still have great flavors.

Since then I've lowered my cholesterol count. My blood pressure has dropped twenty points. I'm not confused or hungry now. I'm healthier *and* I've lost a bunch of pounds. I'm back to discovering new ways to prepare the great food we all enjoy in the Southwest.

Now it's your turn to get on the low salt and less fat wagon. You can do it and still savor those wonderful southwestern flavors.

I have no intention of giving you a dissertation on what to eat or not to eat. My goal is to offer you a chance to reduce your salt, fat, and cholesterol levels while still enjoying the

❖

flavor of the food you're preparing and eating.

As Stephen Sapienza mentioned in his note, in July of 1994 the Center for Science in the Public Interest presented a report that claimed Mexican-style food was extremely high in fat and salt. This is a fact that I had been aware of for several years. Ironically, at the time this report came out I was working on this cookbook and Northland was in the chute to publish it. You might say our timing was perfect. Our product—the recipes in this cookbook—offers a broad selection of foods made with far less salt and fat than traditionally prepared recipes. In other words, in the following pages you will find an opportunity to live a healthier and better life and still eat what you enjoy most.

In the "Nutritional Facts Per Serving" displayed with the ingredients for Black Bean Frijoles (p. xii), you will see what happens with only a few minor modifications. The flavor, quality, quantity, and preparation is the same. But sodium has been reduced from 103 to 58 milligrams per serving, cholesterol has been reduced from 8 to 4 milligrams per serving, fat has been reduced from 5.7 to 2.5 grams per serving, saturated fat has been reduced from 2.0 to 0.4 grams per serving, and the percentage of calories from fat was lowered from 31 to 17.

Every recipe in the cookbook has changed from the original structure. I haven't taken the ax to all the fat, or you and I would have ended up with bland, boring food. What I've done, though, is removed unnecessary fat, such as chicken skin, extra trim from beef, etc.; occasionally altered the preparation; and substituted low-fat and low-salt ingredients for traditional ones. Canola oil is used instead of lard or higher-fat oils; vegetable oil spread is used instead of butter, mar-

## Black Bean Frijoles
### (traditional)

¼ cup bacon grease

½ cup diced cooked chicken

½ cup chopped onion

2 cloves garlic, minced

1 pound dried black beans,
sorted and washed

3 cups chicken stock

2 cups water

½ teaspoon oregano

½ teaspoon salsa habanero

¼ teaspoon salt

NUTRITIONAL FACTS PER SERVING

| | |
|---|---|
| Calories (kcal) | 160.9 |
| Cholesterol (mg) | 6 |
| Sodium (mg) | 104 |
| Total fat (g) | 5.7 |
| Saturated fat (g) | 2.0 |
| % Calories from fat | 31 |

## Black Bean Frijoles
### (modified, see p. 66)

1 tablespoon canola oil

½ cup diced cooked chicken

½ cup chopped onion

2 cloves garlic, minced

1 pound dried black beans,
sorted and washed

3 cups Low-Salt Chicken Stock,
see recipe p. 51

1 cup water

½ teaspoon oregano

½ teaspoon salsa habanero

¼ teaspoon salt substitute

NUTRITIONAL FACTS PER SERVING

| | |
|---|---|
| Calories (kcal) | 130.7 |
| Cholesterol (mg) | 4 |
| Sodium (mg) | 56 |
| Total fat (g) | 2.5 |
| Saturated fat (g) | 0.4 |
| % Calories from fat | 17 |

garine, or shortening; Neufchâtel cheese is substituted for cream cheese; low-sodium salt substitute replaces salt; packaged egg substitute replaces eggs; and Mock Sour Cream (see p. 53) takes the place of store-bought sour cream. Additionally, I've used turbinado (raw) sugar, which is healthier because it lacks the chemicals used to process regular sugar. I've worked hard to allow the flavors to stay close to or at the original levels designed for the recipes.

Oftentimes keeping the flavor high has meant including more chiles and spices—and more flavorful ones—

than usual. You may or may not know of the particular chiles used in these recipes, but you should acquaint yourselves with them and have a good supply on hand if you would like to cook healthy southwestern food often. They are quite common and can be purchased in many places. Probably the best way to become familiar with them is to take a tour of a local Latin market or the international food section of a supermarket. If you don't find the fresh items you're looking for, the canned variety will do nicely. I'm not one for canned prepared foods, but if canned, diced, or whole chiles are easier to find and/or to use, I'm all for it.

On this subject, there are several ways chile products and associated spices and herbs are packaged. As we've discussed, canned chiles are common as well as canned or bottled sauces such as pimiento, jalapeño, cascabel, habanero, etc. In addition, chile and associated spices such as cumin, oregano, and achiote are available in clear plastic packages, spice bottles, and cans. Dry chiles are available in bulk and clear plastic packages. Fresh chiles, such as New Mexico (mild and hot), California (Anaheim), serrano, jalapeno, and pasilla (ancho), when in season, can be found in most produce sections.

To help you locate some of these items, many of the products used in the recipes are shown in the picture on page xiii.

We have included a mail-order section at the back of this cookbook. The vendors listed there can easily provide the necessary products you need to prepare the recipes.

—BOB WISEMAN

❖ ❖ ❖

# Appetizers

# Black Bean Dip

INGREDIENTS

12 ounces Black Bean Frijoles,
see recipe p. 66

½ cup low-fat mozzarella cheese

½ cup minced scallions

¼ teaspoon sage

2 tablespoons green taco sauce

No-salt tortilla chips

METHOD

In a saucepan, combine frijoles,
cheese, scallions, sage, and taco
sauce. Blend together, then
bring heat up slowly to a simmer. Stir for 1 or 2 minutes.

Serve immediately with
tortilla chips.

Servings: Makes about 2 cups
(about 4 servings)

| NUTRITIONAL FACTS PER SERVING | |
|---|---|
| Calories (kcal) | 34.8 |
| Cholesterol (mg) | 2 |
| Sodium (mg) | 53 |
| Total fat (g) | 1.0 |
| Saturated fat (g) | 0.07 |
| % Calories from fat | 27 |

Pictured: Black Bean Dip and Chile, Radish,
and Queso Dip (see recipe p. 4).

# Chile, Radish, and Queso Dip

❖

INGREDIENTS

½ cup Neufchâtel cheese, warmed

½ cup low-fat cottage cheese

2 tablespoons evaporated skim milk

¼ cup diced green chiles

½ cup diced red bell pepper

3 scallions, minced

4 radishes, diced

1 clove garlic, minced

¼ teaspoon white pepper

1 teaspoon lime juice

Dash oregano

Dash cayenne

1 teaspoon white vinegar

¼ teaspoon salt substitute

Radish rounds and cumin powder for garnish

METHOD

Mix all ingredients except garnish. Refrigerate for 1 to 2 hours, then add garnish before serving.

*Servings: Makes about 2½ cups (about 5 servings)*

| NUTRITIONAL FACTS PER SERVING | |
|---|---|
| Calories (kcal) | 38.9 |
| Cholesterol (mg) | 8 |
| Sodium (mg) | 59 |
| Total fat (g) | 2.3 |
| Saturated fat (g) | 1.4 |
| % Calories from fat | 54 |

# Herbed Chile Dip

INGREDIENTS

2 cups low-fat cottage cheese

½ cup Neufchâtel cheese

1 tablespoon garlic powder

½ teaspoon sage

½ teaspoon cumin

1 tablespoon chili powder

¼ cup minced watercress sprigs

¼ cup minced scallions

¼ cup minced pimiento

METHOD

In a glass or ceramic bowl,
combine all ingredients and
blend until smooth

Refrigerate at least 1 hour.
Serve with red beet tortilla chips
if available.

Note: The "chile" in this recipe's
title is represented by the chili
powder, which is derived from
chiles.

Servings: Makes about 2½ cups
(about 5 servings)

| NUTRITIONAL FACTS PER SERVING | |
|---|---|
| Calories (kcal) | 46.6 |
| Cholesterol (mg) | 5 |
| Sodium (mg) | 108 |
| Total fat (g) | 1.6 |
| Saturated fat (g) | 0.9 |
| % Calories from fat | 25 |

# Potato Skins with Chile Poblano

INGREDIENTS

6 medium potatoes, baked
1 hour at 400° F.

3 fresh poblano chiles,
deveined and seeded

1 cup Neufchâtel cheese

½ cup minced celery

1 clove garlic, minced

1 teaspoon minced candied
ginger root

¼ teaspoon white pepper

1 cup Mock Sour Cream,
see recipe p. 53

Cilantro and paprika to garnish

METHOD

Preheat oven to 400 degrees F.

Cut baked potatoes in half
lengthwise and scoop out potato pulp, leaving ¼ inch of pulp
attached to skin; avoid breaking
skin. Save potato pulp for other
uses. Place potato skins on large
baking sheet skin side down and
bake for 5 minutes. Remove
from oven to cool. Reduce oven
heat to warm.

Soak chiles in warm water for
15 minutes to soften. Dry, then
mince them. In a ceramic or
glass bowl, combine chiles,
Neufchâtel cheese, celery, garlic,
ginger root, and white pepper.
Let this filling set for 3–5 minutes to blend flavors.

| NUTRITIONAL FACTS PER SERVING | |
| --- | --- |
| Calories (kcal) | 97.2 |
| Cholesterol (mg) | 8 |
| Sodium (mg) | 113 |
| Total fat (g) | 2.4 |
| Saturated fat (g) | 1.5 |
| % Calories from fat | 22 |

Reheat oven to 400 degrees F.

Fill each potato skin with an equal amount of filling. Arrange on a large baking sheet and bake for 10 minutes. Remove from oven and let cool for 5–10 minutes. Cut in half across short side to make 24 pieces.

Ladle Mock Sour Cream into each potato skin, garnish with cilantro and paprika, and serve.

*Servings*: 12

# Ruidoso Rainbows

INGREDIENTS

8 ounces Neufchâtel cheese

3 tablespoons 1% milk

1 teaspoon lime juice

1 tablespoon tequila

½ teaspoon cumin

¼ teaspoon white pepper

¼ teaspoon turmeric

½ teaspoon chili powder

¼ teaspoon oregano

½ teaspoon onion flakes

¼ teaspoon coriander seed, crushed

¼ teaspoon salt substitute

½ cup diced green chiles

¼ cup diced pimiento

¼ teaspoon cayenne

6 whole scallions

6 large low-fat flour tortillas

| NUTRITIONAL FACTS PER SERVING | |
|---|---|
| Calories (kcal) | 17.4 |
| Cholesterol (mg) | 15 |
| Sodium (mg) | 165 |
| Total fat (g) | 5.7 |
| Saturated fat (g) | 3.0 |
| % Calories from fat | 40 |

METHOD

In a deep bowl, combine cheese, milk, lime juice, and tequila. Using a fork, mix until a smooth paste is formed. In a mortar, combine cumin, white pepper, turmeric, chili powder, oregano, onion flakes, coriander seed, and salt substitute; grind to a powder to release the oils of the herbs and increase their flavor. Add to cheese mix. Add chiles, pimiento, and cayenne, and blend all together. Spoon onto wax paper, shape into a long roll, and divide into six equal parts.

Roll out a tortilla and spoon one part of mix onto the right side of it. Leave the left quarter of tortilla without mixture. Place a scallion at right edge on the cheese mix.

Roll tortilla from right to left so scallion ends up in the middle. Cut Ruidoso Rainbow into four equal parts and store in a serving dish. Repeat process with remaining tortillas. Refrigerate for at least an hour or overnight to blend spices.

For a spicier flavor, add chopped jalapeño or serrano chiles or double the cayenne. Or you can omit the milk and double the tequila.

*Servings:* 12

# Salsa Fresca

INGREDIENTS

2 large tomatoes, chopped

2 tablespoons minced cilantro

1 cup minced onion

1 scallion, minced

¼ cup diced green chiles

2 serrano chiles, minced

½ teaspoon garlic powder

½ teaspoon cumin

1 teaspoon chili powder

1 teaspoon raspberry vinegar

2 tablespoons canola oil

3 tablespoons lime juice

METHOD

Combine all in a serving dish and refrigerate for several hours or overnight. Serve with blue corn tortilla chips.

*Servings: Makes about 3 cups (about 6 servings)*

| NUTRITIONAL FACTS PER SERVING | |
|---|---|
| Calories (kcal) | 35.2 |
| Cholesterol (mg) | 0 |
| Sodium (mg) | 125 |
| Total fat (g) | 2.4 |
| Saturated fat (g) | 0.2 |
| % Calories from fat | 58 |

# Seviche Matamoros

INGREDIENTS

1 pound  sea bass fillets

¾ cup lime juice

¼ cup tarragon vinegar

½ cup minced scallions

½ cup minced white onions

½ cup minced red bell pepper

1 serrano chile, minced

½ teaspoon turbinado sugar

2 tablespoons canola oil

¼ teaspoon salt substitute

Jicama and no-salt tortilla chips for dipping

METHOD

Wash and dry sea bass fillets and dice them in ½-inch pieces. Place fish in glass or ceramic serving bowl. Pour lime juice over fish; cover and refrigerate for 2–3 hours.

Discard lime juice. Combine remaining ingredients, except the jicama and chips, and add fish. Chill for 15 minutes more in the refrigerator.

Serve with slices of jicama or tortilla chips for dipping.

*Servings: Makes about 3½ cups (about 7 servings)*

| NUTRITIONAL FACTS PER SERVING | |
| --- | --- |
| Calories (kcal) | 64.7 |
| Cholesterol (mg) | 16 |
| Sodium (mg) | 27 |
| Total fat (g) | 3.0 |
| Saturated fat (g) | 0.4 |
| % Calories from fat | 43 |

# Pequito Tunas Triangles

INGREDIENTS

6 ounces tuna in water, drained

¼ cup graham cracker crumbs

3 tablespoons evaporated
skim milk

3 tablespoons egg substitute

3 scallions, minced

¼ cup minced jicama

½ teaspoon mustard powder

½ teaspoon Tabasco sauce

Canola oil for frying

¼ cup Cilantro Salsa,
see recipe p. 46

METHOD

In a large bowl, combine tuna, graham cracker crumbs, skim milk, egg substitute, scallions, jicama, mustard powder, and Tabasco sauce. Mix well, then form into four patties about ½ inch thick.

Heat a large skillet until a drop of water quickly sizzles away. Add enough oil to barely cover skillet. Brown patties evenly on both sides. Let cool, then cut each patty in triangles. Spoon a layer of Cilantro Salsa on each.

Refrigerate, covered, until ready to serve.

*Servings:* 12

*Pictured: Pequito Tunas Triangles.*

| NUTRITIONAL FACTS PER SERVING | |
| --- | --- |
| Calories (kcal) | 43.5 |
| Cholesterol (mg) | 4 |
| Sodium (mg) | 69 |
| Total fat (g) | 1.9 |
| Saturated fat (g) | 0.2 |
| % Calories from fat | 39 |

# Wild Turkey Jerky

## INGREDIENTS

3 pounds turkey breast, skinless

½ cup low-sodium soy sauce

3 tablespoons lemon juice

1 teaspoon ginger powder

2 teaspoons liquid smoke

½ teaspoon cayenne

1 teaspoon garlic powder

½ teaspoon white pepper

¼ teaspoon salt substitute

## METHOD

Cut turkey breast into ½-inch strips and place in a bowl. Combine soy sauce, lemon juice, ginger, liquid smoke, cayenne, garlic powder, white pepper, and salt substitute. Pour marinade over turkey and coat evenly. Let stand for 4 hours.

Preheat oven to 180–200 degrees F. Bake for 6–8 hours or until jerky is stiff and contains little or no moisture.

*Servings: Makes about 60 pieces*

| NUTRITIONAL FACTS PER SERVING | |
|---|---|
| Calories (kcal) | 165.1 |
| Cholesterol (mg) | 82 |
| Sodium (mg) | 179 |
| Total fat (g) | 3.5 |
| Saturated fat (g) | 1.0 |
| % Calories from fat | 20 |

❖  ❖  ❖

# Salads

# Caesar's Salad El Paso

INGREDIENTS

2 anchovies, minced

1 tablespoon Dijon-style mustard

2 cloves garlic, minced

¼ teaspoon chili powder

¼ teaspoon salt substitute

2 tablespoons egg substitute

3 tablespoons balsamic vinegar

1 teaspoon Worcestershire sauce

½ cup canola oil

⅓ teaspoon black pepper, freshly ground

¼ teaspoon Tabasco sauce

1 head romaine lettuce

⅛ cup grated queso fresco (Mexican goat cheese)

1 cup Croutons Mi Casa, see recipe p. 132

METHOD

In a large wooden salad bowl, combine anchovies, mustard, garlic, chili powder, and salt substitute; mash to a pulp with the back of a heavy spoon. Add egg substitute, vinegar, Worcestershire sauce, canola oil, pepper, and Tabasco; whip into dressing. Pour dressing into a cup, leaving residue in bowl.

Tear romaine lettuce into large pieces and place in salad bowl where dressing was mixed. Pour dressing over lettuce and garnish with queso fresco and Croutons Mi Casa.

*Servings*: 8

*Pictured: Caesar's Salad El Paso and Mesa Verde Green Bean and Pepper Salad (see recipe p. 26).*

| NUTRITIONAL FACTS PER SERVING | |
| --- | --- |
| Calories (kcal) | 159.7 |
| Cholesterol (mg) | 4 |
| Sodium (mg) | 132 |
| Total fat (g) | 15.3 |
| Saturated fat (g) | 1.6 |
| % Calories from fat | 84 |

# Crab and Jicama Salad

INGREDIENTS

1 head romaine lettuce,
in bite-size pieces

1 cup julienned jicama

3 scallions, julienned

4 radishes, chopped

2 cups crab meat,
in small chunks

2 tablespoons Chile-Garlic
Vinegar, see recipe p. 44

3 teaspoons canola oil

1 tablespoon lemon juice

½ teaspoon turbinado sugar

METHOD

Combine lettuce, jicama, scallions, radishes, and crab meat in a salad bowl and mix.

In a small glass bowl, add vinegar, canola oil, lemon juice, and sugar. Whip with a fork until well blended. Pour over salad or serve on the side.

*Servings*: 8

| NUTRITIONAL FACTS PER SERVING | |
| --- | --- |
| Calories (kcal) | 61.2 |
| Cholesterol (mg) | 34 |
| Sodium (mg) | 174 |
| Total fat (g) | 2.6 |
| Saturated fat (g) | 0.3 |
| % Calories from fat | 38 |

# Five Pepper Salad

## METHOD

Wash and pat dry butter lettuce leaves. In a large bowl, combine butter lettuce, peppers, onion, and olives. In a blender, combine vinegar, canola oil, scallions, sugar, lime juice, garlic powder, steak sauce, Tabasco, salt substitute, and cornstarch; blend to a creamy purée. Add to salad and toss to coat.

Line a salad bowl with romaine leaves. Add salad. Chill a few minutes before serving.

*Servings*: 8

| NUTRITIONAL FACTS PER SERVING | |
|---|---|
| Calories (kcal) | 177.9 |
| Cholesterol (mg) | 0 |
| Sodium (mg) | 237 |
| Total fat (g) | 15.0 |
| Saturated fat (g) | 1.1 |
| % Calories from fat | 73 |

## INGREDIENTS

1 head butter lettuce leaves

1 red bell pepper, sliced in rings

1 green bell pepper, sliced in rings

1 yellow bell pepper, sliced in rings

1 black bell pepper, sliced in rings

1 orange bell pepper, sliced in rings

1 small red onion, sliced in rings

½ cup green pimiento olives, cut across width

¼ cup white vinegar

½ cup canola oil

¼ cup chopped scallions

2 tablespoons turbinado sugar

1 tablespoon lime juice

1 teaspoon garlic powder

1 teaspoon steak sauce

½ teaspoon Tabasco sauce

¼ teaspoon salt substitute

2 tablespoons cornstarch

Romaine lettuce leaves to garnish

# Jicama-Carrot-Onion Salad

❖

INGREDIENTS

8 large romaine lettuce leaves

1 small jicama, julienned

1 carrot, julienned

1 medium red onion,
sliced in rings

½ cup Sour Cream–Parsley
Dressing, see recipe p. 61

¼ cup slivered almonds

METHOD

Arrange romaine leaves on chilled individual salad plates. In a glass bowl, combine jicama, carrot, and red onion. Add Sour Cream–Parsley Dressing and toss. Distribute equal amounts of salad onto plates. Sprinkle with almonds and serve.

*Servings*: 8

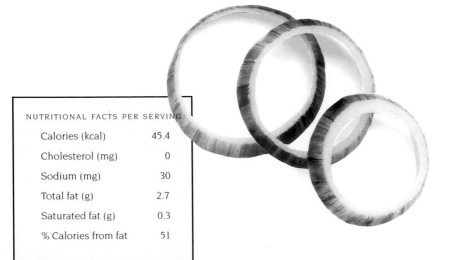

| NUTRITIONAL FACTS PER SERVING | |
| --- | --- |
| Calories (kcal) | 45.4 |
| Cholesterol (mg) | 0 |
| Sodium (mg) | 30 |
| Total fat (g) | 2.7 |
| Saturated fat (g) | 0.3 |
| % Calories from fat | 51 |

# Potato Salad—Southwestern Style

INGREDIENTS

6 medium potatoes,
quartered and boiled

2 boiled eggs

1 medium onion, minced

1 teaspoon raspberry vinegar

2 tablespoons olive oil

1 cup low-fat mayonnaise

¼ cup sweet pickle relish

½ cup Red Chile Sauce—
Enchilada Style, see recipe p. 55

2 tablespoons lime juice

½ teaspoon salt substitute

1 teaspoon dill seed

2 teaspoons mustard powder

¼ teaspoon oregano

¼ teaspoon black pepper

¼ teaspoon garlic powder

Paprika

METHOD

Cut potatoes to size you prefer
and place in a large mixing
bowl. Dice eggs and add to
potatoes. In a blender, combine
all the remaining ingredients
except the paprika, and blend
until smooth. Add to potatoes.
With a wooden spoon, gently
mix ingredients until all pieces
of potato are covered.

Refrigerate 1 hour and serve
garnished with paprika.

Servings: 12

| NUTRITIONAL FACTS PER SERVING | |
|---|---|
| Calories (kcal) | 166.2 |
| Cholesterol (mg) | 24 |
| Sodium (mg) | 190 |
| Total fat (g) | 9.6 |
| Saturated fat (g) | 0.9 |
| % Calories from fat | 51 |

# Romaine-Spinach Salad with Watercress Dressing

INGREDIENTS

1 large head romaine lettuce,
in bite-size pieces

4 bunches spinach leaves

1 small red onion, sliced in rings

½ cup thinly sliced cucumber

2 cloves garlic, minced

Juice of 1 lemon

¼ cup grated Parmesan cheese

¼ cup white vinegar

2 tablespoons egg substitute

½ cup canola oil

½ teaspoon mustard powder

Dash salsa habanero

¼ teaspoon black pepper

½ teaspoon turbinado sugar

½ cup watercress sprigs,
loosely packed

METHOD

In a big salad bowl, combine romaine, spinach, red onion, and cucumber.

In a blender, combine all the remaining ingredients, except half of the watercress. Blend until creamy. Remove dressing to a serving vessel.

Pour half of the dressing over the salad and toss. Garnish with remaining watercress sprigs. Extra dressing can be stored or added to salad.

*Servings:* 8

| NUTRITIONAL FACTS PER SERVING | |
|---|---|
| Calories (kcal) | 166.7 |
| Cholesterol (mg) | 2 |
| Sodium (mg) | 114 |
| Total fat (g) | 15.0 |
| Saturated fat (g) | 1.6 |
| % Calories from fat | 77 |

# Smoked Salmon and Pasilla Chile Salad

METHOD

Combine Tabasco, canola oil, vinegar, lime juice, cilantro, cumin, dill, sugar, and garlic in a deep bowl and whisk together to make a dressing. Cut pasilla chiles into thin strips and add to dressing. Refrigerate for 30 minutes.

In a large bowl, combine bell pepper, radishes, and jicama; mix to blend. With a slotted spoon remove chile strips from dressing and then add to salad mix. Gently fold in diced salmon, being careful not to break fish into smaller pieces.

Place lettuce on chilled salad plates. Add an equal amount of salad to each plate. Garnish with onion. Stir chilled salad dressing and serve separately.

*Servings*: 8

INGREDIENTS

½ teaspoon Tabasco sauce

½ cup canola oil

2 tablespoons white wine vinegar

1 tablespoon lime juice

2 tablespoons chopped cilantro

½ teaspoon cumin

½ teaspoon dill seed

½ teaspoon turbinado sugar

1 clove garlic, minced

2 fresh pasilla chiles

1 small red bell pepper, minced

¼ cup finely chopped radishes

¼ cup diced jicama

1 cup diced smoked Chinook salmon

2 cups chopped lettuce

1 small white onion, sliced in thin rings

| NUTRITIONAL FACTS PER SERVING | |
|---|---|
| Calories (kcal) | 171.5 |
| Cholesterol (mg) | 9 |
| Sodium (mg) | 134 |
| Total fat (g) | 14.6 |
| Saturated fat (g) | 1.2 |
| % Calories from fat | 75 |

# Grilled Chicken and Zucchini Salad

INGREDIENTS

4 chicken breast halves,
skinless and grilled

4 medium zucchini

2 teaspoons salt substitute

1 cup Mock Sour Cream,
see recipe p. 53

1 tablespoon lime juice

1 tablespoon minced
fresh basil leaves

1 teaspoon cumin powder

¼ cup minced onion

Dash black pepper

½ tablespoon paprika

METHOD

Cut 2 grilled chicken breast halves in long strips and set aside for garnish. Chop remaining breasts in bite-size hunks. Shred about half of 1 zucchini and set that aside for garnish.

Cut remaining zucchini in small cubes; add to a colander. Sprinkle zucchini with salt substitute and let stand 15 minutes. Squeeze moisture from zucchini. Combine chicken hunks and remaining ingredients in ceramic or glass bowl. Stir in zucchini cubes. Chill at least one hour.

Serve garnished with shredded zucchini and grilled chicken strips.

| NUTRITIONAL FACTS PER SERVING | |
|---|---|
| Calories (kcal) | 147.2 |
| Cholesterol (mg) | 62 |
| Sodium (mg) | 151 |
| Total fat (g) | 3.1 |
| Saturated fat (g) | 0.9 |
| % Calories from fat | 20 |

*Pictured: Grilled Chicken and Zucchini Salad.*

*Servings: 4*

# Mesa Verde Green Bean and Pepper Salad

INGREDIENTS

½ pound fresh green beans, julienned

1 cup diced red and green bell peppers

1 cup minced white onion

1 teaspoon mustard powder

2 tablespoons Dijon-style mustard

½ teaspoon horseradish

¼ teaspoon white pepper

Dash salt substitute

Dash red chili powder

3 tablespoons canola oil

½ cup dry white wine

6 romaine lettuce leaves

METHOD

In a large bowl, combine green beans, bell peppers, white onion, mustard powder, Dijon-style mustard, horseradish, white pepper, salt, and red chili powder. Mix thoroughly to coat vegetables with spices.

Heat a deep skillet until a drop of water sizzles away. Add canola oil and swirl to cover skillet. Add green bean mixture and sauté until onion starts to become transparent. Add wine and bring to simmer for 5 minutes. Serve warm on romaine lettuce leaves.

*Servings:* 8

| NUTRITIONAL FACTS PER SERVING | |
|---|---|
| Calories (kcal) | 77.2 |
| Cholesterol (mg) | 0 |
| Sodium (mg) | 134 |
| Total fat (g) | 5.6 |
| Saturated fat (g) | 0.4 |
| % Calories from fat | 62 |

❖ ❖ ❖

# Soups and Stews

# Corn Bisque

## INGREDIENTS

3 cups fresh corn kernels

2 cups 1% milk

1 tablespoon egg substitute

1 cup Low-Salt Chicken Stock,
see recipe p. 51

2 stalks celery, diced

¼ cup yellow cornmeal

½ teaspoon white pepper

2 tablespoons lime juice

2 teaspoons orange juice

½ cup evaporated skim milk

Cilantro Salsa, see recipe p. 46

| NUTRITIONAL FACTS PER SERVING | |
|---|---|
| Calories (kcal) | 242.7 |
| Cholesterol (mg) | 6 |
| Sodium (mg) | 145 |
| Total fat (g) | 2.7 |
| Saturated fat (g) | 1.0 |
| % Calories from fat | 9 |

*Pictured: Corn Bisque and Tomato
Bisque (see recipe p. 30).*

## METHOD

In a blender, combine corn, milk,
egg substitute, chicken stock, and
celery; purée and add to a Dutch
oven or stock pot. Cook over
medium heat, stirring often, until
creamy. Remove from heat and
let cool to room temperature.

Strain soup stock into a deep
bowl, pushing as much pulp as
possible through the sieve.
Discard residue from inside of
sieve, then scrape pulp from the
outside into bowl.

Return stock to Dutch oven. Add
cornmeal, white pepper, lime
juice, orange juice, and evaporated milk. Bring to a simmer and,
stirring often, cook for 15 minutes.
Remove from stove and let cool.

Refrigerate at least 4 hours or
overnight. Garnish with Cilantro
Salsa before serving.

*Servings*: 4

# Tomato Bisque

## INGREDIENTS

1½ cups 1% milk

2 tomatoes, diced

1 tablespoon tomato paste

1 teaspoon ancho chile powder

1 clove garlic, minced

1 medium onion, chopped

2 tablespoons masa harina, preferably blue corn

¼ cup chopped pimientos

2 teaspoons turbinado sugar

1 teaspoon lime juice

½ teaspoon horseradish

1 teaspoon vanilla extract

¼ teaspoon salsa habanero

Cilantro Salsa, see recipe p. 46

## METHOD

In a blender, combine milk, tomatoes, tomato paste, ancho chile powder, garlic, and onion; purée. Add to a Dutch oven or stock pot. Bring to a boil, reduce to simmer, and, stirring often, cook over medium heat for 15 minutes. Remove from heat. Let cool to room temperature.

Strain soup stock into a deep bowl, pushing as much pulp through the sieve as possible. Discard residue from inside of sieve and scrape pulp from the outside into bowl.

Return stock to Dutch oven. Add masa harina, pimientos, sugar, lime juice, horseradish, vanilla

| NUTRITIONAL FACTS PER SERVING | |
|---|---|
| Calories (kcal) | 133.8 |
| Cholesterol (mg) | 4 |
| Sodium (mg) | 102 |
| Total fat (g) | 1.5 |
| Saturated fat (g) | 0.7 |
| % Calories from fat | 8 |

extract, and salsa habanero. Bring to a simmer and, stirring often, cook for 15 minutes. Remove from stove and let cool.

Refrigerate at least 4 hours or overnight. Garnish with Cilantro Salsa before serving.

Tomato Bisque and Corn Bisque (p. 28) can be served together in the same bowl, with a partition of aluminum foil to separate them, for a striking effect. See photo on p. 29.

*Servings: 4*

#  Chilled Tomato and Cottage Cheese Soup

❖

INGREDIENTS

2½ cups tomato juice

1 cup 1% milk

1 cup low-fat cottage cheese

2 tablespoons lemon juice

2 teaspoons horseradish

1 teaspoon Tabasco sauce

¼ teaspoon white pepper

4 scallions, chopped

2 tablespoons minced cilantro

METHOD

In a blender, combine tomato juice, milk, cottage cheese, lemon juice, horseradish, Tabasco, and pepper; blend thoroughly. Add the scallions and cilantro and mix.

Refrigerate for 1 hour or overnight.

This is a great soup for a light lunch.

*Servings*: 8

| NUTRITIONAL FACTS PER SERVING | |
|---|---|
| Calories (kcal) | 48.3 |
| Cholesterol (mg) | 3 |
| Sodium (mg) | 415 |
| Total fat (g) | 0.7 |
| Saturated fat (g) | 0.4 |
| % Calories from fat | 12 |

# Bean, Corn, and Squash Caldo

INGREDIENTS

¼ cup canola oil

1 cup chopped onion

2 cloves garlic, minced

4 tomatoes, chopped

2 cups cooked pinto beans

1 cup water

1 tablespoon minced fresh basil

1 teaspoon oregano

¼ teaspoon white pepper

½ cup diced red bell pepper

2 medium acorn squash, peeled, seeded, and chopped in 1-inch pieces

½ cup fresh corn kernels

1 teaspoon achiote

½ teaspoon salt substitute

METHOD

Heat a Dutch oven until a drop of water quickly sizzles away. Add canola oil and coat skillet bottom. Add the onion, garlic, and tomatoes, and sauté until onion is limp. Add beans, water, basil, oregano, and white pepper. Simmer for 20 minutes. Add red bell pepper, squash, corn, achiote, and salt substitute and simmer for 10 more minutes.

Serve hot in soup dishes.

Servings: 8

| NUTRITIONAL FACTS PER SERVING | |
| --- | --- |
| Calories (kcal) | 196.9 |
| Cholesterol (mg) | 0 |
| Sodium (mg) | 12 |
| Total fat (g) | 7.4 |
| Saturated fat (g) | 0.6 |
| % Calories from fat | 32 |

# The Bowl of Red: A Great Chili

INGREDIENTS

1 tablespoon canola oil

3 pounds sirloin tip roast, trimmed of fat and cut in ½-inch cubes

2 tablespoons New Mexico chile powder (mild)

2 tablespoons paprika

3 tablespoons chili powder

1 tablespoon New Mexico chile powder (hot)

5 tablespoons cumin

¼ teaspoon oregano

1 cup chopped onion

4 cloves garlic, minced

3 cups Low-Salt Chicken Stock, see recipe p. 51

1 cup Low-Salt Beef Stock, see recipe p. 50

1 teaspoon Tabasco sauce

½ teaspoon salt substitute

¼ cup cola-flavored beverage

Salsa habanero, for heat

METHOD

Heat a large pot or Dutch oven until a drop of water quickly sizzles away. Add canola oil to coat bottom of pan. Add a third of the sirloin tip cubes and cook until water from meat is almost evaporated. With a slotted spoon, remove meat to a bowl; repeat process with remaining meat, one-third at a time. Remove pot from heat and pour off excess fat and water. Then return all meat to the pot.

In a mortar, combine New Mexico chile powder (mild and hot), paprika, chili powder,

*continued on p. 36*

*Pictured: The Bowl of Red: A Great Chili.*

cumin, and oregano; grind to blend. In a blender, combine onion, garlic, chicken stock, and beef stock and purée.

Reheat the pot, adding contents from blender, and bring to a low boil. Reduce to a simmer and cook for 45 minutes. Add spices from mortar and simmer, covered, for 2 hours. Do not stir the pot. (If you stir chili too much, the meat becomes tough and you lose some of the spice flavors. You just won't have good chili—you can ride herd on that statement.)

Remove cover. At this point, stir once or twice, scraping the sides of the pot. Add Tabasco, salt substitute, cola beverage, and 2 drops of salsa habanero. Stir in and taste. If not hot enough, add a drop or 2 more of salsa habanero.

Serve "hot from the pot." Be sure you have plenty of beer handy.

*Servings*: 8

| NUTRITIONAL FACTS PER SERVING | |
|---|---|
| Calories (kcal) | 432.3 |
| Cholesterol (mg) | 112 |
| Sodium (mg) | 203 |
| Total fat (g) | 19.0 |
| Saturated fat (g) | 5.3 |
| % Calories from fat | 40 |

# Socorro Caldillo

INGREDIENTS

2 pounds beef bottom round

¼ cup canola oil

1 cup finely chopped onion

2 cups finely chopped tomatoes

2 jalapeño peppers, minced

8 green chiles, cut in
¼-inch strips

1 red bell pepper, cut in
1-inch pieces

3 potatoes, cut in 1-inch pieces

12 ounces light beer,
at room temperature

3 cups Low-Salt Beef Stock,
see recipe p. 50

Crumbled tortilla chips to garnish

METHOD

Remove fat from beef and cut into 1-inch cubes. Heat a Dutch oven or deep skillet until a drop of water quickly sizzles away. Add canola oil and brown the beef cubes on all sides. Add onion, tomatoes, jalapeños, green chiles, red bell pepper, potatoes, beer, and beef stock Reduce heat to a simmer, cover, and cook for about 1 hour or until beef pulls apart with a fork.

Serve in soup bowls with crumbled tortilla chips on top.

*Servings:* 12

| NUTRITIONAL FACTS PER SERVING | |
| --- | --- |
| Calories (kcal) | 227.9 |
| Cholesterol (mg) | 73 |
| Sodium (mg) | 100 |
| Total fat (g) | 7.5 |
| Saturated fat (g) | 2.2 |
| % Calories from fat | 31 |

*Pictured on p. 38, top to bottom: Chile Garlic Vinegar (see recipe p. 44), Cilantro Salsa (p. 46), and Ancho Chile Sauce (p. 41).*

❖ ❖ ❖

# Sauces,
# Stocks,
# and Basics

# Tomato Chile Gravy

INGREDIENTS

2 teaspoons canola oil

1 cup diced tomatoes

½ cup diced green chiles

½ cup chopped red onion

½ cup Low-Salt Chicken Stock,
see recipe p. 51

3 tablespoons 1% milk

2 tablespoons Wondra flour

½ cup plain low-fat yogurt

¼ teaspoon cayenne

¼ teaspoon black pepper

METHOD

In a deep skillet, combine canola oil, tomatoes, chiles, and onion. Bring to a simmer over medium heat. Add chicken stock and bring back to simmer.

Combine milk and flour and blend until smooth. Add flour-milk mixture, yogurt, and cayenne to skillet. Bring to a simmer and stir until starting to thicken. Add pepper before serving.

Serve as a sauce over Chicken Santa Fe, p. 92.

*Servings: Makes 2½–3 cups*

| NUTRITIONAL FACTS PER SERVING | |
| --- | --- |
| Calories (kcal) | 42.4 |
| Cholesterol (mg) | 1 |
| Sodium (mg) | 70 |
| Total fat (g) | 1.6 |
| Saturated fat (g) | 0.3 |
| % Calories from fat | 33 |

# Ancho Chile Sauce

INGREDIENTS

1 cup water

2 cups Low-Salt Chicken Stock, see recipe p. 51

3 tablespoons ancho chile powder

2 tablespoons paprika

2 tablespoons green tomato chile sauce

½ cup minced onion

1 teaspoon cumin

½ teaspoon garlic powder

½ teaspoon oregano

1 tablespoon tomato paste

¼ teaspoon white vinegar

1 teaspoon turbinado sugar

Dash vanilla extract

Dash salt and white pepper

METHOD

In a deep saucepan, combine all ingredients and, stirring constantly, bring to a low boil. Cover and, stirring often, let simmer for 45 minutes.

Serve over enchiladas, tamales, burritos, etc.

Servings: Makes 4 cups

| NUTRITIONAL FACTS PER SERVING | |
|---|---|
| Calories (kcal) | 33.3 |
| Cholesterol (mg) | 0 |
| Sodium (mg) | 154 |
| Total fat (g) | 1.0 |
| Saturated fat (g) | 0.04 |
| % Calories from fat | 23 |

# Chicken Filling

INGREDIENTS

2 tablespoons canola oil

1 medium onion, chopped

4 scallions, minced

1 clove garlic, minced

2 cups diced cooked chicken

¼ teaspoon cayenne

¼ cup coarsely chopped almonds

½ cup green enchilada sauce

METHOD

In a skillet, heat a drop of water until it quickly sizzles away. Add oil to coat skillet. Add onion, scallions, and garlic, and sauté until onion is transparent. Blend in chicken, cayenne, almonds, and sauce. Simmer 10 minutes, stirring occasionally.

This filling is especially good in enchiladas.

*Servings: Makes 3 cups*

| NUTRITIONAL FACTS PER SERVING | |
| --- | --- |
| Calories (kcal) | 75.1 |
| Cholesterol (mg) | 17 |
| Sodium (mg) | 18 |
| Total fat (g) | 4.4 |
| Saturated fat (g) | 0.5 |
| % Calories from fat | 53 |

# Chile Dill Sauce

INGREDIENTS

1 cup low-fat cottage cheese

3 tablespoons 1% milk

¼ cup low-fat mayonnaise

2 tablespoons lime juice

1 cup diced pimientos

1 cup diced green chiles

¼ cup grated cucumber

1 tablespoon dill seed

¼ teaspoon white pepper

1 pinch cayenne

Diced pimiento and
chile to garnish

METHOD

In a deep bowl, combine cottage cheese, milk, mayonnaise, and lime juice; mix thoroughly. Blend in pimientos, chiles, cucumber, dill seed, white pepper, and cayenne. Refrigerate for at least 3 hours or overnight to enhance flavors.

Serve as a sauce over fish, veal, or chicken, or mix with prepared cold pasta shells and serve as a salad or side dish.

Chile Dill Sauce is best pre-made and refrigerated overnight.

*Servings: Makes 4–5 cups*

| NUTRITIONAL FACTS PER SERVING | |
|---|---|
| Calories (kcal) | 68.1 |
| Cholesterol (mg) | 5 |
| Sodium (mg) | 151 |
| Total fat (g) | 2.7 |
| Saturated fat (g) | 0.6 |
| % Calories from fat | 18 |

# Chile-Garlic Vinegar

INGREDIENTS

6 cloves garlic, slightly mashed

4 dried japon chiles
(or arbol chiles)

1 dried chile serrano

1 stick cinnamon

1 quart white vinegar

METHOD

To two clean pint containers add equal portions of garlic, japon chiles, serrano chiles, and cinnamon. Pour 1 pint of vinegar in each. Store in a cool dark place for 4 weeks. *Do not disturb*.

Strain vinegar and return to either a single quart container or two pint jars. Add fresh chiles and cinnamon stick to each.

*Servings: Makes one quart*

| NUTRITIONAL FACTS PER SERVING | |
| --- | --- |
| Calories (kcal) | 12.2 |
| Cholesterol (mg) | 0 |
| Sodium (mg) | 27 |
| Total fat (g) | 0.02 |
| Saturated fat (g) | 0 |
| % Calories from fat | 2 |

# Chimayo Chile Salad Dressing

INGREDIENTS

¼ cup lime juice

2 tablespoons canola oil

½ teaspoon garlic powder

¼ teaspoon black pepper

1 tablespoon dry sherry

¼ cup raspberry vinegar

½ teaspoon chile chimayo powder (or mild chile New Mexico powder)

¼ teaspoon turbinado sugar

METHOD

In a blender, combine all ingredients and blend. Serve over salads or use as a marinade.

It's sweet. It's sour. It's an outstanding salad dressing.

Servings: Makes 1½ cups

| NUTRITIONAL FACTS PER SERVING | |
| --- | --- |
| Calories (kcal) | 36.9 |
| Cholesterol (mg) | 0 |
| Sodium (mg) | 3 |
| Total fat (g) | 3.5 |
| Saturated fat (g) | 0.2 |
| % Calories from fat | 80 |

# Cilantro Salsa

INGREDIENTS

2 tablespoons diced green chiles

1 clove garlic, minced

¼ cup minced white onion

Dash salsa habanero

½ cup chopped cilantro,
lightly packed

3 tablespoons canola oil

1 tablespoon lime juice

1 tablespoon Mock Sour Cream,
see recipe p. 53

METHOD

Combine all ingredients in a
blender and purée. Set aside to
cool, or store in a refrigerator for
up to 2 weeks

*Servings: Makes ¾ cup*

| NUTRITIONAL FACTS PER SERVING | |
| --- | --- |
| Calories (kcal) | 101.7 |
| Cholesterol (mg) | 0 |
| Sodium (mg) | 14 |
| Total fat (g) | 10.3 |
| Saturated fat (g) | 0.7 |
| % Calories from fat | 90 |

# Cilantro-Cashew Pesto

INGREDIENTS

2 cloves garlic, minced

½ cup chopped cilantro

¼ cup chopped cashews

2 tablespoons freshly grated
Romano cheese

¾ cup canola oil

1 tablespoon lime juice

⅛ teaspoon white pepper

METHOD

In a blender or salsa maker, add
all ingredients and blend until
thoroughly mixed.

This recipe, the basic sauce for
Lamb Medallions with Cilantro-
Cashew Pesto, p. 107, is wonderful with any pasta, grilled chicken
breasts, or, after thinning with
2 tablespoons of red wine vinegar, as a salad dressing.

Refrigerate covered with a
thin layer of olive oil. Use within
3 weeks.

*Servings: Makes about 1½ cups*

| NUTRITIONAL FACTS PER SERVING | |
| --- | --- |
| Calories (kcal) | 142.0 |
| Cholesterol (mg) | 1 |
| Sodium (mg) | 12 |
| Total fat (g) | 15.2 |
| Saturated fat (g) | 1.4 |
| % Calories from fat | 94 |

# Drunken Porker Filling

INGREDIENTS

2 tablespoons canola oil

2 fresh green chiles,
seeded and deveined

3 cloves garlic

1 cup chopped onion

¼ cup raisins

½ cup diced red and
green bell peppers

3 scallions, minced

1 teaspoon oregano

½ teaspoon salt substitute

½ teaspoon white pepper

1 cup Mexican-style tomato sauce

3 cups cooked and
diced pork loin chops

½ ounces light beer,
at room temperature

¼ cup tequila

METHOD

Heat a skillet until a drop of
water quickly sizzles away. Add
canola oil to coat skillet. Slice
chiles in short strips (across the
pod). Add chiles, garlic, onion,
raisins, bell peppers, and scallions to skillet and sauté.

Add oregano, salt substitute,
white pepper, tomato sauce,
pork, beer, and tequila and bring
to a simmer. Cover and, stirring
occasionally, cook until most
liquid has evaporated and filling
is thick.

*Servings: Makes 6–7 cups*

| NUTRITIONAL FACTS PER SERVING | |
|---|---|
| Calories (kcal) | 156.0 |
| Cholesterol (mg) | 34 |
| Sodium (mg) | 193 |
| Total fat (g) | 7.3 |
| Saturated fat (g) | 1.8 |
| % Calories from fat | 42 |

# Fajita Marinade

INGREDIENTS

½ cup papaya nectar

2 tablespoons low-sodium soy sauce

¼ cup dry sherry

1 tablespoon balsamic vinegar

Dash Tabasco sauce

½ teaspoon garlic powder

1 teaspoon turbinado sugar

METHOD

In a blender, combine all ingredients until thoroughly mixed. Refrigerate.

This marinade can be used with beef, poultry, or pork.

*Servings: Makes 1 cup*

| NUTRITIONAL FACTS PER SERVING | |
|---|---|
| Calories (kcal) | 24.0 |
| Cholesterol (mg) | 0 |
| Sodium (mg) | 133 |
| Total fat (g) | 0 |
| Saturated fat (g) | 0 |
| % Calories from fat | 1 |

# Low-Salt Beef Stock

## INGREDIENTS

4 pounds small beef bones,
neck, tail, etc.

4 cloves garlic, mashed

2 large carrots, sliced thin

2 stalks celery, chopped

1 large onion, quartered

3 cups red wine

3 bay leaves

4 sprigs parsley

4 peppercorns, crushed
in a mortar

½ teaspoon liquid smoke

16 cups water

## METHOD

Preheat oven to 300 degrees F.
Remove remaining meat and fat
from bones. In a large roasting
pan, combine bones, garlic, 1 sliced
carrot, ½ cup celery, and 2 onion
quarters. Roast for ½ hour, turning
bones once. Place hot bones in a
deep stew pot. Deglaze the roasting pan by adding the wine and,
with a wooden spoon, scraping
bottom of pan. Add deglazed vegetables and juices to stew pot; fol-
low with remaining ingredients.
Bring to a boil. Skim foam from
surface. Reduce to a simmer and
cover the pot; cook for 2 hours.

Let broth cool. Skim off fat.
Remove meat and save for other
uses. Strain broth and refrigerate
overnight. Skim off the fat that
coagulates after refrigeration.

Will store in refrigerator for up to
2 weeks. The smoke flavor adds
just enough of a change to make
this stock stand out from others.

*Servings: Makes about 16 cups*

NUTRITIONAL FACTS PER SERVING
Nutritional facts
unavailable for
this recipe.

# Low-Salt Chicken Stock

INGREDIENTS

1 chicken, skinned and
cut in sections

4 cloves garlic, minced

2 large carrots,
sliced ¼-inch thick

1 stalk celery, sliced ¼-inch thick

1 green pepper, chopped

1 large onion, quartered

8 cloves

3 bay leaves

4 stalks parsley

1 cinnamon stick

4 peppercorns, crushed
in a mortar

20 cups water

METHOD

Wash chicken pieces and place in
a deep stew pot. Add remaining
ingredients. Bring to a boil. Skim
off foam, being careful to leave
parsley stems in stew pot.
Reduce to a slow simmer, then
cover pot and cook about 45 minutes or until chicken is tender.

Let broth cool. Skim off fat.
Remove meat from broth and
save for other uses. Strain broth
and refrigerate overnight. Skim
off fat that coagulates while
refrigerated.

Will store in refrigerator for up
to 2 weeks. This is a basic stock
made without salt.

NUTRITIONAL FACTS PER SERVING
Nutritional facts
unavailable for
this recipe.

*Servings: Makes about 16 cups*

# Low-Salt Fish Stock

INGREDIENTS

18 cups water

2 pounds fish bones

1 leek, chopped

1 cup chopped celery

8 sprigs cilantro

1 medium onion, chopped

3 cloves garlic, mashed

2 bay leaves

METHOD

In a Dutch oven or stew pot, bring the water to a boil. Add the fish and boil until foam appears on surface. Skim off foam and add other ingredients. Cover and simmer for 30 minutes. Let cool, then strain and discard solids.

Use as directed in recipes.

Will store, refrigerated in a tightly sealed jar, for 1 week.

*Servings: Makes about 16 cups*

NUTRITIONAL FACTS PER SERVING

Nutritional facts unavailable for this recipe.

# Mock Sour Cream

INGREDIENTS

2 cups low-fat cottage cheese

½ cup low-fat buttermilk

METHOD

Combine ingredients in a
blender and process until
smooth, scraping down sides of
container often.

Refrigerate and serve when
needed. Ideal topping for
enchiladas.

*Servings: Makes 2½ cups*

| NUTRITIONAL FACTS PER SERVING | |
|---|---|
| Calories (kcal) | 23.5 |
| Cholesterol (mg) | 2 |
| Sodium (mg) | 122 |
| Total fat (g) | 0.4 |
| Saturated fat (g) | 0.2 |
| % Calories from fat | 14 |

# Orange and Chile Sauce

INGREDIENTS

2 cups Low-Salt Chicken Stock,
see recipe p. 51

2 tablespoons New Mexico
chile powder (mild)

1 tablespoon green taco sauce

1 tablespoon minced cilantro

1 tablespoon cornstarch

¼ cup orange juice

¼ cup evaporated skim milk

Dash salt substitute and
black pepper

METHOD

In a saucepan, combine chicken
stock, chile powder, green taco
sauce, and cilantro and bring to a
simmer. In a small mixing bowl,
combine corn starch, orange
juice, evaporated skim milk, salt,
and pepper. Mix until well blended
and add to simmering sauce.
Continue to simmer until sauce
starts to thicken. Remove from
heat, cool, and refrigerate.

Ideal sauce for chicken enchiladas and burritos.

*Servings: Makes 3 cups*

| NUTRITIONAL FACTS PER SERVING | |
| --- | --- |
| Calories (kcal) | 51.5 |
| Cholesterol (mg) | 1 |
| Sodium (mg) | 91 |
| Total fat (g) | 1.1 |
| Saturated fat (g) | 0 |
| % Calories from fat | 18 |

# Red Chile Sauce—Enchilada Style

INGREDIENTS

4 tablespoons canola oil

2 tablespoons Wondra flour

¾ cup New Mexico chile powder (mild)

½ teaspoon cayenne

4 cups Low-Salt Chicken Stock, see recipe p. 51

3 cloves garlic, crushed

1 teaspoon oregano

4 ounces Mexican-style tomato sauce

½ teaspoon salt substitute

METHOD

Heat a Dutch oven or stew pot until a drop of water sizzles away. Add canola oil and Wondra flour and stir to make a light roux. Add remaining ingredients and bring to a low boil. Reduce to a simmer and cook for 20 minutes, stirring occasionally. Remove from heat and let cool to room temperature.

Refrigerate for immediate use or store in freezer.

*Servings: Makes about 4 cups*

| NUTRITIONAL FACTS PER SERVING | |
| --- | --- |
| Calories (kcal) | 91.6 |
| Cholesterol (mg) | 0 |
| Sodium (mg) | 126 |
| Total fat (g) | 7.3 |
| Saturated fat (g) | 0.5 |
| % Calories from fat | 70 |

# Salsa Basil

INGREDIENTS

2 tablespoons heavy cream

½ cup plain low-fat yogurt

½ cup Low-Salt Chicken Stock,
see recipe p. 51

1 tablespoon canola oil

3 tablespoons dry white wine

1 tablespoon dried basil (or
2 tablespoons fresh, chopped)

3 cloves garlic, minced

¼ cup dried tomatoes,
chopped coarse

¼ teaspoon white pepper

Pinch cayenne

METHOD

In a cold saucepan, combine all ingredients. Bring to a low boil. Reduce to a light simmer and cook until sauce starts to thicken. Remove from heat and bring to room temperature. Store in refrigerator until ready to use.

This sauce is delicious over pasta (see Salsa Basil con Pasta, p. 136) or over chicken breasts (see Pollo Escondido, p. 113).

*Servings: Makes 1½ cups*

| NUTRITIONAL FACTS PER SERVING | |
| --- | --- |
| Calories (kcal) | 97 |
| Cholesterol (mg) | 12 |
| Sodium (mg) | 102 |
| Total fat (g) | 6.8 |
| Saturated fat (g) | 2.3 |
| % Calories from fat | 61 |

# Salsa Flamenco

### INGREDIENTS

¼ cup olive oil

1 cup sliced mushrooms

1 cup coarsely chopped
dried tomatoes

¼ cup sliced black olives

1 clove garlic, minced

2 scallions, chopped

½ teaspoon Tabasco sauce

½ cup Marsala wine

Pinch white pepper, to taste

### METHOD

Heat a deep skillet until a drop
of water sizzles away and then
add olive oil. Add mushrooms,
tomatoes, olives, garlic, and
scallions and sauté until mushrooms are limp. Add Tabasco,
Marsala, and pepper. Cover and
simmer for 5 minutes.

Serve over pompano, snapper,
swordfish, and tuna.

*Servings: Makes 2 cups*

| NUTRITIONAL FACTS PER SERVING | |
|---|---|
| Calories (kcal) | 192.2 |
| Cholesterol (mg) | 0 |
| Sodium (mg) | 383 |
| Total fat (g) | 15.2 |
| Saturated fat (g) | 2.0 |
| % Calories from fat | 67 |

# Salsa Mole

INGREDIENTS

4 tablespoons canola oil

2 tablespoons sesame seeds

¼ cup almond slivers,
raw preferred

2 tablespoons unsalted
dry-roasted peanuts

2 tablespoons raisins

¾ cup bread crumbs

2 low-fat corn tortillas, crumbled

3 whole cloves

Pinch anise seed

1 tomato, seeded and chopped

½ cup chopped onion

2 cloves garlic, minced

2 cups Low-Salt Chicken Stock,
see recipe p. 51

2 ounces semisweet chocolate

1 cinnamon stick

1 tablespoon turbinado sugar

2 teaspoons salt substitute

½ cup warm water

METHOD

Heat a deep skillet until a drop
of water quickly sizzles away.
Add 2 tablespoons of the canola
oil to coat skillet. Fry sesame
seeds, almonds, peanuts, and
raisins for 5 minutes. Add bread
crumbs, tortillas, cloves, anise
seed, tomato, onion, and garlic
and sauté for 5 more minutes.
Remove from heat and let cool
slightly, then add all to a
blender, including the chicken
stock. Blend to purée. Strain
mixture through a course sieve
and then blend again, adding
the residue from the strainer.
Continue until you have a purée
and all of the mix has cleared
the strainer. Remove to a bowl
to free blender for next step.

In the skillet, add the remaining 2 tablespoons of canola oil and bring up to moderate heat. Add chocolate, cinnamon stick, sugar, and salt and cook for no more than 2 minutes. Remove to blender and add ½ cup warm water. Blend until nearly a purée (use more water if needed). Strain and discard cinnamon stick residue.

Combine both mixtures in skillet and simmer until thick.

Salsa Mole is used in many dishes; see Mole Poblano, p. 110.

*Servings: Makes 5 cups*

| NUTRITIONAL FACTS PER SERVING | |
| --- | --- |
| Calories (kcal) | 243.7 |
| Cholesterol (mg) | 0 |
| Sodium (mg) | 168 |
| Total fat (g) | 14.7 |
| Saturated fat (g) | 2.6 |
| % Calories from fat | 52 |

# Salsa Tequila

INGREDIENTS

2 tablespoons canola oil

¼ cup diced green chiles

1 jalapeño pepper, minced

½ cup coarsely chopped pickled cactus (*nopalito*)

¼ cup minced onion

3 ounces tequila

1 tablespoon lime juice

½ cup orange juice

2 tablespoons Neufchâtel cheese

1 tablespoon egg substitute

1 teaspoon turbinado sugar

½ teaspoon salt substitute

METHOD

Heat a skillet until a drop of water quickly sizzles away. Add enough canola oil to coat skillet. Add chiles, jalapeño, cactus, and onion and sauté until onion starts to turn clear. Turn off heat.

In a blender, combine tequila, lime juice, orange juice, cheese, egg substitute, sugar, and salt substitute and blend until smooth. Add blended mix to skillet and reheat over low flame, stirring constantly. Simmer and continue to stir until juice starts to thicken.

This sauce goes well with many meat dishes; see especially Javelina Brochettes with Salsa Tequila, p. 104.

| NUTRITIONAL FACTS PER SERVING | |
| --- | --- |
| Calories (kcal) | 80.0 |
| Cholesterol (mg) | 3 |
| Sodium (mg) | 72 |
| Total fat (g) | 4.4 |
| Saturated fat (g) | 0.8 |
| % Calories from fat | 48 |

*Servings: Makes 1½ cups*

# Sour Cream–Parsley Dressing

INGREDIENTS

3 tablespoons green taco sauce

½ cup chopped parsley, loosely packed

½ cup Mock Sour Cream, see recipe p. 53

1 tablespoon grated Parmesan cheese

2 tablespoons balsamic vinegar

⅓ cup water

1 tablespoon canola oil

Dash Tabasco sauce

Dash onion powder

METHOD

Combine all ingredients in a blender and purée. Refrigerate.

This dressing goes well with any green salad.

*Servings: Makes 1½ cups*

| NUTRITIONAL FACTS PER SERVING | |
| --- | --- |
| Calories (kcal) | 20.7 |
| Cholesterol (mg) | 1 |
| Sodium (mg) | 45 |
| Total fat (g) | 1.4 |
| Saturated fat (g) | 0.2 |
| % Calories from fat | 60 |

❖  ❖  ❖

# Side Dishes

# Spanish Rice

INGREDIENTS

2 tablespoons canola oil

1 cup uncooked white rice

1 medium onion, chopped

1 small red bell pepper, chopped

1 small green bell pepper, chopped

½ teaspoon garlic powder

2 tablespoons tomato paste

4 cups Low-Salt Chicken Stock, see recipe p. 51

½ cup diced green chiles

METHOD

Heat a skillet until a drop of water quickly sizzles away. Add canola oil to coat pan. Add rice and brown lightly. Remove rice to a small bowl. To the skillet, add onion and bell peppers and sauté. Add garlic powder, tomato paste, chicken stock, and chiles. Return rice to the pan. Reduce heat to a simmer; cover and cook until all moisture is absorbed and rice is done (approximately 25–30 minutes).

*Servings*: 8

| NUTRITIONAL FACTS PER SERVING | |
|---|---|
| Calories (kcal) | 106 |
| Cholesterol (mg) | 0 |
| Sodium (mg) | 70 |
| Total fat (g) | 3.9 |
| Saturated fat (g) | 0.3 |
| % Calories from fat | 33 |

*Pictured on p. 62: Lima and Pinto Beans (see recipe p. 65) and Spanish Rice.*

# Lima and Pinto Beans

see recipe p. 51

INGREDIENTS

½ cup dried baby lima beans, sorted and washed

½ cup dried pinto beans, sorted and washed

3 cups Low-Salt Chicken Stock, see recipe p. 51

2 tablespoons tomato paste

1 tablespoon molasses

¼ cup chopped pimiento

2 cloves garlic, minced

½ cup minced onion

¼ teaspoon black pepper

Salt substitute

METHOD

In a saucepan or Dutch oven, combine lima beans, pinto beans, and chicken stock. Bring to a boil and cook for 5 minutes. Reduce to simmer, cover, and cook for ½ hour.

Add remaining ingredients. Simmer for 2 hours, adding water to keep a good consistency if needed.

*Servings:* 8

| NUTRITIONAL FACTS PER SERVING | |
| --- | --- |
| Calories (kcal) | 108 |
| Cholesterol (mg) | 0 |
| Sodium (mg) | 59 |
| Total fat (g) | 0.6 |
| Saturated fat (g) | 0.1 |
| % Calories from fat | 5 |

# Black Bean Frijoles

## INGREDIENTS

1 tablespoon canola oil

½ cup diced cooked chicken

½ cup chopped onion

2 cloves garlic, minced

1 pound dried black beans, sorted and washed

3 cups Low-Salt Chicken Stock, see recipe p. 51

1 cup water

½ teaspoon oregano

½ teaspoon salsa habanero

¼ teaspoon salt substitute

## METHOD

Heat a deep skillet or Dutch oven until a drop of water quickly sizzles away. Add canola oil and chicken and sauté until chicken is light brown. Add onion and garlic and sauté until onion is limp. Add black beans, chicken broth, and 1 cup water. Bring to a low boil and add oregano, salsa habanero, and salt substitute. Boil for 5 minutes. Reduce to simmer. Cover and simmer for 2 to 2½ hours or until beans are soft. Add extra water if needed.

Remove from heat and let cool. Put half of the frijoles in a blender, purée, and combine with original mixture.

Reheat to desired consistency and, if you like, serve with shredded low-fat cheese sprinkled on top.

*Servings:* 12

| NUTRITIONAL FACTS PER SERVING | |
| --- | --- |
| Calories (kcal) | 130.7 |
| Cholesterol (mg) | 4 |
| Sodium (mg) | 58 |
| Total fat (g) | 2.5 |
| Saturated fat (g) | 0.4 |
| % Calories from fat | 17 |

# Cheese and Egg Burrito

❖

**METHOD**

In a mixing bowl, combine egg substitute, red bell pepper, scallions, and salt and pepper. Heat a skillet until a drop of water quickly sizzles away. Add canola oil and the mixture from the bowl. Cook until eggs are well scrambled. Remove from heat and set aside in a separate bowl covered with foil to keep warm. Wash and dry skillet and return it to stove.

In a saucepan, bring Orange and Chile Sauce to a simmer. Immerse a flour tortilla in sauce to make it more pliable; then add a fourth of the egg mixture and a fourth of the cheese to center of tortilla. Fold tortilla into a burrito and place in skillet. Turn heat under skillet to low. Repeat process with remaining tortillas. Bring heat to medium, cover skillet, and cook until cheese starts to melt. Serve covered with a ladle of sauce.

*Servings:* 4

**INGREDIENTS**

1 cup egg substitute

¼ cup diced red bell pepper

2 scallions, minced

Dash salt substitute and white pepper

1 tablespoon canola oil

1½ cups Orange and Chile Sauce, see recipe p. 54

4 large low-fat flour tortillas

½ cup shredded low-fat mozzarella

| NUTRITIONAL FACTS PER SERVING | |
|---|---|
| Calories (kcal) | 259.4 |
| Cholesterol (mg) | 6 |
| Sodium (mg) | 403 |
| Total fat (g) | 10.1 |
| Saturated fat (g) | 1.1 |
| % Calories from fat | 35 |

# Hacienda Hash Browns

INGREDIENTS

2 medium potatoes,
peeled and quartered

1 small onion, diced

¼ cup diced green chiles

2 scallions, chopped

1 tablespoon egg substitute

1 tablespoon masa corn flour

¼ teaspoon garlic powder

¼ teaspoon black pepper

3 tablespoons 1% milk

2½ tablespoons canola oil

METHOD

Finely chop potatoes. In a large bowl, add potatoes, onion, green chiles, scallions, egg substitute, masa, garlic powder, pepper, milk, and 1 tablespoon of the canola oil. Blend thoroughly.

In a large skillet or a griddle, bring heat up until a drop of water quickly sizzles away. Add remaining 1½ tablespoons of canola oil and thoroughly coat cooking surface. Pour potato mixture over oil. Cook until slightly browned, turn, and repeat. Mix browned potato into itself, then brown again. Repeat this procedure until you have a good blend of browned potatoes.

Serve in triangle wedges. Great as a brunch side dish—fast and easy to prepare.

*Servings:* 4

| NUTRITIONAL FACTS PER SERVING | |
| --- | --- |
| Calories (kcal) | 146.0 |
| Cholesterol (mg) | 1 |
| Sodium (mg) | 20 |
| Total fat (g) | 7.3 |
| Saturated fat (g) | 0.6 |
| % Calories from fat | 44 |

# Reynaldo's Spiced Sweet Carrots

INGREDIENTS

2 pounds carrots,
sliced crosswise

¼ cup canola oil

3 stalks celery, chopped

1 green pepper, diced

3 scallions, cut in 1-inch pieces

3 tablespoons tomato paste

1 teaspoon oregano

½ cup brown sugar, crumbled

½ cup Low-Salt Chicken Stock,
see recipe p. 51

1 teaspoon mustard powder

1 tablespoon Worcestershire
sauce

¼ teaspoon white pepper

METHOD

Cook carrots in water to cover
until tender. Drain and set aside
in a deep serving bowl. Add oil
to a saucepan and bring to moderate heat. Add celery, green
pepper, and scallions and sauté
for 5 minutes. Add tomato paste,
oregano, brown sugar, chicken
stock, mustard, Worcestershire
sauce, and pepper.

Pour heated sauce mixture over
carrots. Bring to room temperature and then refrigerate for at
least 1 hour or overnight.

This makes a great side dish that
can be prepared ahead of time.

*Servings:* 8

| NUTRITIONAL FACTS PER SERVING | |
| --- | --- |
| Calories (kcal) | 178.2 |
| Cholesterol (mg) | 0 |
| Sodium (mg) | 160 |
| Total fat (g) | 7.3 |
| Saturated fat (g) | 0.5 |
| % Calories from fat | 35 |

# Pinto Bean Frijoles

## INGREDIENTS

1 pound dried pinto beans, sorted and washed

2 cloves garlic, minced

3 cups water (to cover beans)

1 teaspoon cumin

½ teaspoon oregano

1 teaspoon salt substitute

¼ cup minced extra-lean ham

¼ cup minced onion

## METHOD

In a Dutch oven, combine pinto beans, garlic, and 3 cups of water, or just enough to cover beans. Bring to a boil and then reduce to simmer. Add cumin, oregano, and salt substitute. Simmer, covered, for 2 hours, adding more water if needed. Add ham and onion and bring back to simmer. Cook for 30 minutes.

Remove from heat and let cool. Put half of mixture in a blender, purée, and return to main mixture.

Reheat to desired consistency and serve with shredded low-fat cheese sprinkled on top.

Frijoles will store refrigerated for up to a week. Frozen they will store for up to three months.

*Servings*: 8

| NUTRITIONAL FACTS PER SERVING | |
| --- | --- |
| Calories (kcal) | 190.7 |
| Cholesterol (mg) | 1 |
| Sodium (mg) | 53 |
| Total fat (g) | 1.0 |
| Saturated fat (g) | 0.2 |
| % Calories from fat | 5 |

# Pisto Manchego–Style Stewed Peppers and Squash

INGREDIENTS

⅓ cup canola oil

3 cups coarsely chopped onion

1 large crookneck squash, diced in ½-inch pieces

1 medium zucchini, diced in ½-inch pieces

2 large bell peppers, chopped

½ cup light beer, at room temperature

½ cup tomato paste

3 tablespoons egg substitute

1 teaspoon salt substitute

½ teaspoon white pepper

Dash salsa habanero

¼ cup chopped cilantro for garnish

METHOD

Heat a deep skillet until a drop of water quickly sizzles away. Add canola oil. Add onion, crookneck squash, zucchini, peppers, and beer. Cook for about 2 minutes, reduce heat to a slight simmer, cover, and cook for 15 minutes more.

Add tomato paste, egg substitute, salt substitute, white pepper, and salsa habanero. Simmer for 5 minutes.

Serve garnished with cilantro. This is a great vegetable dish with beef steaks or roasts.

Servings: 8

| NUTRITIONAL FACTS PER SERVING | |
| --- | --- |
| Calories (kcal) | 142.4 |
| Cholesterol (mg) | 0 |
| Sodium (mg) | 144 |
| Total fat (g) | 9.7 |
| Saturated fat (g) | 0.7 |
| % Calories from fat | 58 |

# Pork and Black Bean Burritos

INGREDIENTS

2 cups cubed lean pork shoulder

½ teaspoon garlic powder

1 teaspoon cumin

2 tablespoons canola oil

1 small onion, diced

3 stalks celery, chopped

2 serrano chiles, finely minced

1 cup water

2 cups Black Bean Frijoles,
see recipe p. 66

Vegetable spray

8 large low-fat flour tortillas

4 scallions, finely chopped

1 cup grated low-sodium
cheddar cheese

½ cup diced red bell peppers

Red Chile Sauce—Enchilada
Style, see recipe p. 55

METHOD

In a glass bowl, combine pork
shoulder cubes, garlic powder,
and cumin; mix to coat all sides
of meat.

Heat a skillet until a drop of
water quickly sizzles away. Add
canola oil to cover skillet. Add
onion and celery and sauté until
onion is transparent. Add pork,
serrano chiles, and water and
simmer for 20 minutes or until
water is nearly gone. Reduce
heat to keep warm.

In a separate pan, heat Black
Bean Frijoles just until they
are heated through. Remove
from heat.

| NUTRITIONAL FACTS PER SERVING | |
| --- | --- |
| Calories (kcal) | 351.9 |
| Cholesterol (mg) | 32 |
| Sodium (mg) | 367 |
| Total fat (g) | 16.9 |
| Saturated fat (g) | 4.1 |
| % Calories from fat | 43 |

Preheat oven to 350 degrees F.

Spray a casserole dish with vegetable spray. Lay out a tortilla and fill its middle with 2 tablespoons bean mixture and 2 tablespoons pork mixture. Fold in sides of burrito and place seam side down in casserole. Repeat until all burritos are finished. Sprinkle scallions, cheese, and red bell peppers over burritos. Bake in oven until cheese melts, about 15 minutes.

While burritos are baking, heat Red Chile Sauce. Serve burritos with a coating of sauce.

*Servings*: 8

# Puerto Penasco Spicy Fish Tacos

❖

INGREDIENTS

1 pound fish fillets (sea bass
and snapper work well)

Canola oil for frying

1 medium onion, sliced in rings

2 cloves garlic, minced

½ cup diced green chiles

8 low-fat flour tortillas

2 cups shredded low-sodium
colby cheese

2 cups shredded romaine lettuce

2 cups chopped tomatoes,
drained

½ cup diced radishes

½ cup chopped scallions

Green taco sauce

METHOD

Clean and dry fish fillets and cut
in ½-inch strips.

Heat a skillet until a drop of
water quickly sizzles away. Add
enough canola oil to coat skillet. Add fish and cook until firm
(about a minute on each side).
Remove fish to a paper towel to
drain and cover with foil to
keep warm.

To skillet, add onion, garlic, and
green chiles; cook until onion is
limp. Remove sautéed vegetables to a bowl and cover with
foil to retain heat. Wash and dry
skillet and return to stove. Lay a
tortilla flat in skillet and heat
until brown spots start to
appear (about 15–20 seconds).

| NUTRITIONAL FACTS PER SERVING | |
| --- | --- |
| Calories (kcal) | 280.0 |
| Cholesterol (mg) | 33 |
| Sodium (mg) | 265 |
| Total fat (g) | 9.0 |
| Saturated fat (g) | 2.1 |
| % Calories from fat | 29 |

Turn tortilla and heat again.
Remove tortilla to a plate.
Spoon some fish into center of
tortilla, add sautéed vegetables,
sprinkle cheese on top, then add
romaine, tomatoes, radishes,
scallions, and green taco sauce.
Shape into a taco, secure with a
toothpick, and wrap in foil to
retain moisture. Repeat process
until all tortillas are used.

Remove from foil and serve
accompanied with frijoles
refritos, or refried beans.

*Servings*: 8

# Sonoran Green Rice

INGREDIENTS

½ cup canola oil

2 cups uncooked white rice

½ cup water

3 fresh green chiles,
seeded and deveined

1 clove garlic, minced

1 small onion, chopped

½ cup fresh corn kernels

4 cups Low-Salt Chicken Stock,
see recipe p. 51

1 teaspoon achiote

Salt substitute, to taste

¼ cup thinly sliced radishes

METHOD

Heat a Dutch oven until a drop
of water quickly sizzles away.
Add canola oil to coat skillet.
Add rice and lightly brown.
Remove Dutch oven from heat.

In a blender, combine water,
chiles, garlic, and onion and
purée. Add purée to rice and
return pan to heat. Bring to a
simmer. Add corn, chicken stock,
achiote, and salt substitute.
Cover and simmer for about 40
minutes or until rice is done.

Serve garnished with radishes.

*Servings:* 12

| NUTRITIONAL FACTS PER SERVING | |
| --- | --- |
| Calories (kcal) | 211.0 |
| Cholesterol (mg) | 0 |
| Sodium (mg) | 128 |
| Total fat (g) | 9.6 |
| Saturated fat (g) | 0.7 |
| % Calories from fat | 41 |

# Spanish Trail Twice-Baked Spuds

❖

## METHOD

Preheat oven to 400 degrees F.

Bake whole potatoes for 45 minutes. Remove and let cool. Slice potatoes in half lengthwise. Form 4 shells by scooping out most of the potato pulp, being careful not to pierce the skin. Remove the potato pulp to a blender and add the cream cheese, onion, egg substitute, Tabasco, chili powder, milk, and pepper. Blend until smooth. Add cilantro and mix.

Add equal amounts of potato mix to the 4 reserved skins, heaping in the skins to form a tall mound. Enclose skins in aluminum foil, leaving the tops open.

Reheat oven to 300 degrees F. Bake potatoes for 25 minutes.

*Servings*: 4

## INGREDIENTS

2 potatoes, with skins

¼ cup Neufchâtel cheese

¼ cup minced onion

¼ cup egg substitute

2 dashes Tabasco sauce

1 teaspoon chili powder

2 tablespoons 1% milk

¼ teaspoon white pepper

2 tablespoons chopped cilantro

| NUTRITIONAL FACTS PER SERVING | |
|---|---|
| Calories (kcal) | 165.3 |
| Cholesterol (mg) | 9 |
| Sodium (mg) | 147 |
| Total fat (g) | 3.4 |
| Saturated fat (g) | 0.7 |
| % Calories from fat | 18 |

# Spicy Beef Tacos

INGREDIENTS

Canola oil for frying

1 pound lean ground beef

1 medium onion, cut in thin rings

1 clove garlic, minced

½ cup diced green chiles

2 serrano chiles, minced

8 low-fat corn tortillas

½ cup grated Romano cheese

2 cups shredded romaine lettuce leaves

2 cups chopped tomatoes

½ cup coarsely chopped jicama

½ cup chopped scallions

Red Chile Sauce—Enchilada Style, see recipe p. 55

METHOD

Heat a skillet until a drop of water quickly sizzles away. Add enough canola oil to coat skillet. Add ground beef and cook. Remove to paper towel to drain and cover with foil to retain heat.

To skillet, add onion, garlic, green chiles, and serrano chiles and cook until onion is limp. Remove sautéed vegetables to a bowl and cover with foil to retain heat. Wash and dry skillet and return to stove.

Lay a tortilla flat in skillet and heat until brown spots start to show (about 15–20 seconds). Turn tortilla and heat on other side. Remove tortilla and keep warm until all are heated. Spoon some beef into center of each tortilla and add sautéed vege-tables; sprinkle with Romano cheese; add romaine, tomatoes, jicama, and scallions; top with Red Chile Sauce.

*Servings:* 8

| NUTRITIONAL FACTS PER SERVING | |
|---|---|
| Calories (kcal) | 262.0 |
| Cholesterol (mg) | 49 |
| Sodium (mg) | 448 |
| Total fat (g) | 13.8 |
| Saturated fat (g) | 5.6 |
| % Calories from fat | 47 |

# Texican Sweet and Sour Zucchini

## INGREDIENTS

8 medium zucchini

Canola oil for sautéing

4 tablespoons low-sodium soy sauce

4 tablespoons red wine vinegar

½ teaspoon onion powder

4 tablespoons turbinado sugar

1 teaspoon salt substitute

## METHOD

Cut zucchini in half lengthwise, then cut lengths across the middle. You should have 32 pieces about 2 inches long.

Heat a skillet until a drop of water quickly sizzles away. Add enough canola oil to coat skillet. Add soy sauce and sauté zucchini, stirring to coat, for no more than 1½–2 minutes. Reduce to simmer, add vinegar, onion powder, sugar, and salt substitute. Simmer for 3 minutes. Remove pan from heat and bring to room temperature.

Chill in refrigerator for 4 hours before serving.

*Servings*: 8

| NUTRITIONAL FACTS PER SERVING | |
| --- | --- |
| Calories (kcal) | 48.4 |
| Cholesterol (mg) | 0 |
| Sodium (mg) | 264 |
| Total fat (g) | 1.8 |
| Saturated fat (g) | 0.1 |
| % Calories from fat | 31 |

# Whistlin' Dixie Creole Rice and Red Beans

❖

### INGREDIENTS

1 pound dried red kidney beans, sorted and washed

1 teaspoon baking soda

4 large tomatoes, chopped

1 large onion, chopped

2 tablespoons canola oil

1 bay leaf

1 teaspoon cumin

1 teaspoon achiote

¼ teaspoon crumbled dry red chiles

½ teaspoon salt substitute

8 cups cooked rice

### METHOD

To a stew pot or Dutch oven, add beans and cover with cold water 1 inch above surface of beans. Bring to a boil and cook for 5 minutes. Remove from heat, add baking soda, and stir until all bubbles are gone. Return to heat and simmer for 1 hour.

Add tomatoes, onion, canola oil, bay leaf, cumin, achiote, red chiles, and salt substitute. Simmer for 1½ hours. Add extra water if needed.

Serve over rice.

*Servings*: 8

| NUTRITIONAL FACTS PER SERVING | |
|---|---|
| Calories (kcal) | 439.4 |
| Cholesterol (mg) | 0 |
| Sodium (mg) | 169 |
| Total fat (g) | 4.8 |
| Saturated fat (g) | 0.5 |
| % Calories from fat | 10 |

❖ ❖ ❖

# Entrées

# Basque-Style Stuffed Peppers

INGREDIENTS

2 tablespoons olive oil

1 serrano chile, chopped

2 tablespoons diced pimiento

1 medium yellow onion,
chopped

½ cup chopped mushrooms

1 pound ground lamb

½ teaspoon sage

½ teaspoon rosemary

1 teaspoon chopped mint

½ cup light beer,
at room temperature

¼ cup bread crumbs

8 large bell peppers
(red preferred)

1 cup Low-Salt Chicken Stock,
see recipe p. 51

½ cup chopped scallions

1 clove garlic, minced

4 Roma tomatoes,
seeded and chopped

¼ cup chopped parsley

½ cup dry red wine

1 teaspoon Wondra flour

*Pictured: Basque-Style Stuffed Peppers.*

METHOD

Heat a Dutch oven until a drop
of water quickly sizzles away.
Add olive oil to cover skillet.
Add serrano chile, pimiento,
onion, and mushrooms; sauté
until onions are transparent.
Add lamb and cook until meat is
browned. In a bowl, blend sage,
rosemary, mint, beer, and bread
crumbs. Add lamb mixture and
blend to make a filling. Reserve
cooking juices.

Preheat oven to 200 degrees F.

Cut around bell pepper stems
and remove seeds; save stems.
Spoon in filling, taking care not
to break peppers; replace

*continued on p. 84*

stems. Reheat Dutch oven; add chicken stock and bring to a simmer. Place stuffed peppers, stems up, in broth, cover, and steam for 30 minutes. Remove peppers to a plate and place in oven to keep warm.

To the liquid in the Dutch oven, add scallions, garlic, tomatoes, parsley, wine, reserved cooking juices, and flour. Bring sauce to a simmer and cook for 10 minutes.

Discard pepper stems and spoon sauce over peppers.

The best way to enjoy Basque-Style Stuffed Peppers is to serve them with thick chunks of sourdough bread ripped from the loaf and an old-fashioned water glass (or bota bag) full of hearty red wine.

*Servings*: 8°

| NUTRITIONAL FACTS PER SERVING | |
|---|---|
| Calories (kcal) | 218.1 |
| Cholesterol (mg) | 41 |
| Sodium (mg) | 331 |
| Total fat (g) | 12.4 |
| Saturated fat (g) | 4.0 |
| % Calories from fat | 49 |

# Catfish Jambalaya

### METHOD

Heat a large skillet until a drop of water quickly sizzles away. Add olive oil and swirl to coat bottom of pan. Add onion, garlic, bell peppers, and celery; sauté until onion is limp and slightly clear. Add parsley and thyme and cook for 5 minutes, stirring often. Add tomatoes, tomato paste, pasilla chile, pimiento, cayenne, Tabasco, wine, filé gumbo, chicken stock, and rice. Bring to a simmer, then cover and cook for 20 minutes or until rice is plump.

Add catfish and mix gently. Cover and simmer for 15 more minutes. Transfer to a large a preheated bowl. Garnish with cilantro and paprika and serve.

*Servings:* 8

| NUTRITIONAL FACTS PER SERVING | |
| --- | --- |
| Calories (kcal) | 211.1 |
| Cholesterol (mg) | 36 |
| Sodium (mg) | 169 |
| Total fat (g) | 8.5 |
| Saturated fat (g) | 1.5 |
| % Calories from fat | 33 |

### INGREDIENTS

2 tablespoons olive oil

½ cup onion slices

2 cloves garlic, minced

1 cup diced red and green bell peppers

½ cup diced celery

¼ cup minced parsley

½ teaspoon thyme

2 large tomatoes, coarsely chopped

2 tablespoons tomato paste

1 fresh pasilla chile, seeded and chopped

¼ cup chopped pimiento

½ teaspoon cayenne

1 tablespoon Tabasco sauce

1 cup dry white wine

2 teaspoons filé gumbo

2 cups Low-Salt Chicken Stock, see recipe p. 51

1 cup uncooked rice

1 pound boneless catfish fillets (or redfish or sea bass), cut in 1-inch pieces

¼ cup minced cilantro

1 teaspoon paprika

# Chicken Enchiladas

INGREDIENTS

3 tablespoons canola oil

3 chicken breast halves, skinless

½ cup chopped onion

2 cloves garlic, minced

1 whole diced pimiento

1 cup Neufchâtel cheese

2 whole scallions,
diced in ½-inch pieces

3 cups Ancho Chile Sauce,
see recipe p. 41

8 low-fat corn tortillas

1 cup Mock Sour Cream,
see recipe p. 53

Diced pimientos and scallions

METHOD

In a saucepan, heat canola oil over moderate heat. Add chicken breasts and cook until done. Remove from heat and let cool. Slice in thin strips, then cut to 1-inch lengths.

Combine onion, garlic, and pimento in skillet and sauté until onion is translucent. Let cool. Add cheese and scallions; blend.

Preheat oven to 375 degrees F.

Spread ½ cup of Ancho Chile Sauce in bottom of a nine-by-thirteen-inch casserole dish. In a skillet, heat remaining 2½ cups Ancho Chile Sauce to a simmer.

| NUTRITIONAL FACTS PER SERVING | |
|---|---|
| Calories (kcal) | 238.6 |
| Cholesterol (mg) | 38 |
| Sodium (mg) | 337 |
| Total fat (g) | 11.2 |
| Saturated fat (g) | 3.0 |
| % Calories from fat | 41 |

Pictured: *Chicken Enchiladas.*

*continued on p. 88*

Immerse a tortilla in the sauce to make it more pliable and then spoon equal portions of filling and chicken into the center of the tortilla. Roll the filled tortilla and place in casserole dish.

Fill and arrange remaining enchiladas evenly in dish and spread 1 cup of warmed Ancho Chile Sauce over top. Cover with foil and bake 10–15 minutes. Remove from oven and discard foil. Place each enchilada on a plate, spoon Ancho Chile Sauce over it, and top with 1 or 2 tablespoons of Mock Sour Cream.

Serve garnished with diced pimientos and scallions.

*Servings:* 8

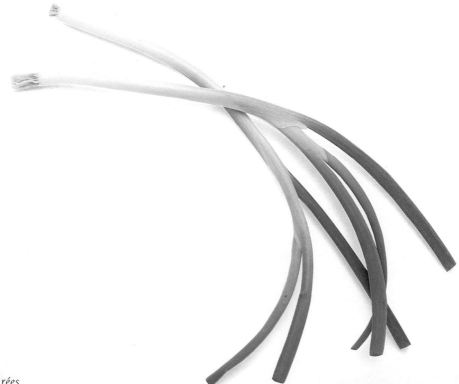

# Chile Verde Roberto

## METHOD

Trim all excess fat from pork and cut meat in bite-size cubes (not too small). In a large Dutch oven, heat water to boil. Add the pork, a fourth of the garlic, ½ tablespoon of the cumin, and the star anise. Boil for 20–30 minutes to remove fat. Using a slotted spoon, remove meat to a colander and rinse in hot water to remove more fat. Remove star anise from the pot and discard liquid. Rinse and dry pot.

Heat canola oil in Dutch oven. Add the pork and brown on all sides. Add the remaining garlic, bell pepper, tomatoes, green chiles, cilantro, ground cloves, remaining 2½ tablespoons cumin, lime juice, chicken stock, and salt. Simmer for 2 hours.

Serve in soup bowls accompanied by Colorful Jalapeño Cornbread (see recipe on p. 130).

*Servings*: 8

## INGREDIENTS

3 pounds lean pork shoulder

5 cups water

4 cloves garlic, crushed

3 tablespoons cumin

1 whole star anise

1 tablespoon canola oil

1 bell pepper, seeded and chopped

6 medium tomatoes, seeded and chopped

2 cups diced green chiles

¼ cup chopped cilantro

¼ teaspoon ground cloves

¼ cup lime juice

2 cups Low-Salt Chicken Stock, see recipe p. 51

½ teaspoon salt substitute

| NUTRITIONAL FACTS PER SERVING | |
|---|---|
| Calories (kcal) | 351.6 |
| Cholesterol (mg) | 112 |
| Sodium (mg) | 139 |
| Total fat (g) | 20.3 |
| Saturated fat (g) | 6.1 |
| % Calories from fat | 52 |

# Chicken Ole! Ole!

INGREDIENTS

4 chicken breast halves, skinless

4 chicken thighs, skinless

½ cup all-purpose flour

½ teaspoon white pepper

½ teaspoon cayenne

2 tablespoons canola oil

16 small mushrooms, quartered

8 scallions, quartered with tops

2 cloves garlic, minced

1½ cups dry white wine

8 cherry tomatoes

1 cup Mock Sour Cream,
see recipe p. 53

1 tablespoon achiote

Minced fresh basil, to garnish

METHOD

Rinse chicken in water and pat dry. In a paper bag, combine flour, white pepper, and cayenne. Place a piece of chicken in the bag, hold closed, and shake to coat the chicken. Remove chicken to a dry surface and continue until all chicken has been thoroughly floured. Reserve flour mix.

Preheat oven to 200 degrees F. and place a large serving dish inside to warm.

Heat a deep skillet or Dutch oven until a drop of water quickly sizzles away. Add canola oil and spread to cover skillet. Brown chicken on all sides and

| NUTRITIONAL FACTS PER SERVING | |
|---|---|
| Calories (kcal) | 472.6 |
| Cholesterol (mg) | 112 |
| Sodium (mg) | 399 |
| Total fat (g) | 16.2 |
| Saturated fat (g) | 3.2 |
| % Calories from fat | 31 |

remove to warm plate in oven. Maintain skillet on stove over medium heat.

Add mushrooms, scallions, and garlic to skillet and sauté for 2–3 minutes. In a bowl, combine wine and 2 tablespoons of reserved flour mixture and blend; then add to skillet. Discard remaining flour. Add cherry tomatoes, Mock Sour Cream, and achiote. Cover and simmer for 15 minutes or until sauce starts to thicken.

Pour sauce over chicken, garnish with basil, and serve.

This makes a wonderful brunch or early dinner entrée.

*Servings*: 4

# Chicken Santa Fe with Tomato Chile Gravy

INGREDIENTS

4 chicken breast halves,
boned and skinless

½ cup lime juice

½ cup low-fat cream cheese

4 scallions, chopped

2 teaspoons minced pimiento

2 cloves garlic, minced

4 green olives, minced

½ teaspoon oregano

¼ teaspoon cumin

¼ teaspoon white pepper

1 cup Low-Salt Chicken Stock,
see recipe p. 51

2 cups Tomato Chile Gravy,
see recipe p. 40

METHOD

Flatten each chicken breast between sheets of wax paper using a mallet and a rolling pin. Place in a baking pan and sprinkle with lime juice to marinate. Cover and refrigerate 1 hour.

Preheat oven to 375 degrees F.

In a bowl, combine cream cheese, scallions, pimiento, garlic, olives, oregano, cumin, and pepper. Mix well.

Remove chicken breasts to a cutting board and pat dry. Discard lime marinade. Spread a layer of mixed ingredients on each chicken breast. Roll breasts and secure each with toothpicks.

| NUTRITIONAL FACTS PER SERVING | |
| --- | --- |
| Calories (kcal) | 258.0 |
| Cholesterol (mg) | 80 |
| Sodium (mg) | 392 |
| Total fat (g) | 10.4 |
| Saturated fat (g) | 4.0 |
| % Calories from fat | 39 |

Place prepared chicken breasts in a baking pan. Add chicken broth to pan. Seal pan with aluminum foil. Bake for 30 minutes. Remove foil and bake for 15 minutes more.

Serve by placing a bit of Tomato Chile Gravy on each plate, place a chicken roll on the gravy, and top with more gravy.

*Servings*: 4

# Chile Elk Steaks

❖

## INGREDIENTS

8 ½-pound elk steaks

1 large onion, minced

4 cloves garlic, minced

1 teaspoon salsa habanero

2 tablespoons minced crystallized ginger

8 green chiles

Vegetable spray

## METHOD

Wash steaks in cold water and pat dry. Score both sides of steaks with a sharp knife, being careful not to cut too deep.

In a mixing bowl, combine onion, garlic, salsa habanero, and ginger to make a poultice. Spread equal amounts of poultice on both sides of steaks, making sure to get some into scored areas. Split open chiles and remove all seeds and membranes.

Tear off 8 pieces of extra heavy-duty aluminum foil and spray each piece on one side with vegetable spray. Place an elk steak in the middle of the oiled side of each piece of foil. Lay a

| NUTRITIONAL FACTS PER SERVING | |
|---|---|
| Calories (kcal) | 347.5 |
| Cholesterol (mg) | 165 |
| Sodium (mg) | 146 |
| Total fat (g) | 4.3 |
| Saturated fat (g) | 1.6 |
| % Calories from fat | 12 |

chile on top of the steak and fold aluminum from one side at a time to totally enclose steak (the object is to seal aluminum tight enough to retain juices). Repeat until all steaks are wrapped in foil.

Fire up a charcoal or gas grill. Spray cooking surface of grill with vegetable oil. When grill is hot, place foil-wrapped steaks top side down on grill and, with grill top closed, cook for 15 minutes. Turn steaks over (sealed top should now be facing you). With grill top closed, cook for 10 more minutes.

When serving steaks, be careful not to spill juices. Serve, using juices as a sauce.

*Servings:* 8

# Drunken Porker Enchiladas

INGREDIENTS

3 tablespoons canola oil

8 low-fat corn tortillas

3 cups Red Chile Sauce—
Enchilada Style, see recipe p. 55

½ cup light beer,
at room temperature

Vegetable spray

2 cups Drunken Porker Filling,
see recipe p. 48

1½ cups grated low-sodium
cheddar cheese

Chopped scallions and tomatoes

METHOD

Heat a skillet until a drop of water quickly sizzles away. Add canola oil to coat skillet. Fry tortillas on both sides but remove them before they become crisp. Set aside on paper towels to drain.

Add Red Chile Sauce and beer to skillet and bring to a low simmer.

Preheat oven to 350 degrees F.

Spray a long shallow casserole dish with vegetable oil. Immerse a tortilla in the sauce to coat on both sides. Lay tortilla in casserole dish and spoon about 3 tablespoons of Drunken Porker Filling down the center. Roll the

| NUTRITIONAL FACTS PER SERVING | |
|---|---|
| Calories (kcal) | 333.1 |
| Cholesterol (mg) | 40 |
| Sodium (mg) | 360 |
| Total fat (g) | 19.0 |
| Saturated fat (g) | 4.3 |
| % Calories from fat | 51 |

tortilla and place, flap side down, at one end of casserole dish. Repeat process with remaining tortillas until all are filled and placed in casserole. Reserve 1 cup of sauce and pour remaining sauce over tortillas. Sprinkle grated cheddar cheese on top of enchiladas. Cover casserole with foil and bake for 20 minutes.

To serve, pour reserved cup of sauce over enchiladas and garnish with scallions and tomatoes.

*Servings*: 8

# Fillet Brochettes

INGREDIENTS

4 pounds fillet of beef,
cut in 1-inch cubes

24 pearl onions

16 cherry tomatoes

1 teaspoon cumin

1 teaspoon oregano

1 teaspoon sage

½ teaspoon black pepper

Vegetable spray, for basting

1 tablespoon paprika

1 tablespoon New Mexico
chile powder (mild)

1 teaspoon ancho chile powder

4 tablespoons canola oil

2 cloves garlic, minced

2 tomatillos,
husked and chopped

2 tomatoes,
seeded and chopped

1 bay leaf

½ teaspoon white pepper

¼ teaspoon salt substitute

2 cups water

METHOD

On 8 metal or bamboo skewers, alternate beef, onion, and to-mato pieces.

In a mortar, combine cumin, oregano, sage, and black pepper. Sprinkle spice mix evenly on skewered brochettes. Spray with vegetable oil. Wrap in foil and refrigerate for 1 hour.

In a saucepan, add paprika, New Mexico chile powder, ancho chile powder, canola oil, garlic, tomatillos, tomatoes, bay leaf, white pepper, salt substitute, and water. Stirring occasionally, bring to a low boil and then reduce to simmer. Cook for 30 minutes or until sauce starts to thicken slightly. Remove from heat and discard bay leaf. When slightly cool, purée sauce in a blender; then return to stove to keep warm.

Prepare a charcoal or gas grill.

Grill brochettes close to charcoal or gas flame, spraying with vegetable oil at each turn, until they are brown on all sides.

Serve with a covering of chile sauce.

*Servings*: 8

| NUTRITIONAL FACTS PER SERVING | |
|---|---|
| Calories (kcal) | 366.3 |
| Cholesterol (mg) | 115 |
| Sodium (mg) | 190 |
| Total fat (g) | 19.5 |
| Saturated fat (g) | 5.5 |
| % Calories from fat | 48 |

# Golden Lamb Chops

### INGREDIENTS

2 cups water

8 lamb loin chops, trimmed of fat and sinew

1 tablespoon Tabasco sauce

1 tablespoon white vinegar

2 tablespoons mustard powder

¼ cup honey

1 cup dry white wine

½ teaspoon garlic powder

Dash cayenne

Vegetable spray

### METHOD

In a deep skillet or Dutch oven, combine water, lamb chops, Tabasco, and white vinegar. Bring to a low boil, reduce to simmer, and cook for 45 minutes.

Meanwhile, in a saucepan, combine mustard powder, honey, wine, garlic powder, and cayenne to make a baste. Bring to a simmer and then reduce heat to just warm.

Preheat oven to 350 degrees F.

Remove lamb chops from water and pat dry. Brush on both sides with the baste. Spray a large casserole dish with vegetable oil and add the chops. Bake uncovered in oven for 15 minutes. Baste again, then bake for another 30 minutes.

Remove from oven and serve. Remaining baste can be used as a sauce if desired.

*Servings*: 8

| NUTRITIONAL FACTS PER SERVING | |
|---|---|
| Calories (kcal) | 328.2 |
| Cholesterol (mg) | 73 |
| Sodium (mg) | 66 |
| Total fat (g) | 22.6 |
| Saturated fat (g) | 9.5 |
| % Calories from fat | 62 |

# Huachinango Vera Cruz
## (Red Snapper Vera Cruz Style)

INGREDIENTS

8 fillets red snapper
(or orange roughy)

½ teaspoon white pepper

¼ cup lime juice

All-purpose flour, for dredging

1 teaspoon chili powder

¼ cup canola oil

2 cloves garlic

½ large onion, cut in thin rings

1 large red bell pepper,
cut in thin rings

1 large green bell pepper,
cut in thin rings

1 bay leaf

½ teaspoon thyme

½ teaspoon cumin

4 ripe tomatoes,
peeled and chopped

2 cups Low-Salt Fish Stock,
see recipe p. 52

¼ cup minced green olives

1 fresh pasilla chile, julienned

1 teaspoon balsamic vinegar

METHOD

Wash and pat dry fillets.

Combine white pepper and lime juice to make a marinade. Place fillets on a large flat plate and sprinkle both sides with marinade. Let stand for 20 minutes; pat dry with a paper towel. In a deep dish, combine flour and chili powder and lightly dredge both sides of fillets.

Preheat oven to 200 degrees F. and place a large serving plate in oven to warm.

Heat a skillet or Dutch oven until a drop of water sizzles away. Add canola oil and spread to coat skillet. Fry fillets on both

*continued on p. 102*

sides until light brown. Remove fillets and drain, retaining oil in pan. Keep fillets in a warm oven on a warm serving plate.

To reserved oil, add whole garlic cloves and sauté until light brown. Remove garlic and sauté onion and red and green bell peppers until limp. Add bay leaf, thyme, cumin, and tomatoes and stir until mixture is well blended. Add fish stock and bring to a boil. Add olives, pasilla chile, and vinegar and reduce heat to simmer for 15 minutes.

Remove warmed plate from oven and pour sauce over fillets. Serve immediately.

*Servings:* 8

| NUTRITIONAL FACTS PER SERVING | |
|---|---|
| Calories (kcal) | 231.5 |
| Cholesterol (mg) | 41 |
| Sodium (mg) | 193 |
| Total fat (g) | 9.3 |
| Saturated fat (g) | 0.9 |
| % Calories from fat | 38 |

*Pictured: Huachinango Vera Cruz*
*(see recipe p. 101).*

# Javelina Brochettes with Salsa Tequila

INGREDIENTS

3 pickled jalapeño peppers

¼ cup canola oil

12 ounces light beer,
at room temperature

1 small onion, minced

2 cloves garlic, minced

2 teaspoons lime juice

3 tablespoons Salsa Mole,
see recipe p. 58

1½ pounds javelina meat (or
lean pork shoulder or lamb
shoulder), cut in 1-inch cubes

16 cherry tomatoes

2 zucchini, cut in 1-inch rounds

16 large pimiento-stuffed
green olives

1 medium jicama,
cut in ½-inch cubes

2 teaspoons salsa picante

Vegetable spray

Salsa Tequila, see recipe p. 60

METHOD

In a blender, combine jalapeños, canola oil, beer, onion, garlic, lime juice, and Salsa Mole. Blend until marinade is smooth. In a deep glass bowl, combine javelina cubes and marinade. Mix well to coat meat. Refrigerate for 4–6 hours or overnight.

You will need to use two skewers for each brochette in order to keep them from rolling.

Remove javelina meat from marinade, and reserve marinade as a baste. Pierce a tomato with two skewers, add a cube of javelina, a round of zucchini, javelina, olive, javelina, zucchini, jicama, olive, and finish with a tomato at the end. Repeat process until all meat and vegetables are used up.

Fire up a charcoal or gas grill. When it's ready, wipe the grill surface with a cloth soaked in canola oil to keep brochettes from sticking. Add salsa picante to marinade and mix thoroughly. Spray all sides of brochettes with vegetable spray and baste with marinade, then place on grill. Cook for 3–4 minutes to a side.

Serve accompanied by Salsa Tequila.

*Servings:* 8

| NUTRITIONAL FACTS PER SERVING | |
|---|---|
| Calories (kcal) | 271.3 |
| Cholesterol (mg) | 77 |
| Sodium (mg) | 497 |
| Total fat (g) | 14.8 |
| Saturated fat (g) | 2.9 |
| % Calories from fat | 49 |

# Huachinango San Felipe
## *(San Felipe Red Snapper)*

INGREDIENTS

8 fillets red snapper (or orange roughy), washed and patted dry

¼ cup lime juice

6 egg whites

½ teaspoon vanilla extract

½ cup 1% milk

½ cup masa harina

½ teaspoon celery seed

½ cup canola oil

1½ cups Chile Dill Sauce, see recipe p. 43

4 oranges, quartered

4 limes, quartered

METHOD

In a large dish, sprinkle fillets with half the lime juice on one side, the remaining lime juice on the other. Set aside for 30 minutes to marinate.

In a deep bowl, combine egg whites, vanilla extract, milk, masa harina, and celery seed; mix thoroughly to form a thin batter.

In a deep skillet, add canola oil and bring to a moderate heat. Dip two fillets in the batter and add to skillet. Fry until lightly browned on both sides. Set aside on a heated plate in a warm oven (200 degrees F.). Repeat process for remaining fillets.

Serve covered with Chile Dill Sauce (warmed to room temperature) and garnished with oranges and limes.

*Servings:* 8

| NUTRITIONAL FACTS PER SERVING | |
|---|---|
| Calories (kcal) | 261.6 |
| Cholesterol (mg) | 41 |
| Sodium (mg) | 118 |
| Total fat (g) | 9.2 |
| Saturated fat (g) | 1.0 |
| % Calories from fat | 31 |

# Lamb Medallions with Cilantro-Cashew Pesto

INGREDIENTS

1½ pounds lamb sirloin

½ cup all-purpose flour

½ teaspoon oregano

¼ teaspoon white pepper

1 tablespoon canola oil

1 cup Cilantro-Cashew Pesto, see recipe p. 47

4 sprigs mint leaves, minced

METHOD

Slice lamb sirloin crosswise in ¼-inch medallions (to make 12 medallions). With a cleaver, pound lightly to slightly flatten. Combine flour, oregano, and white pepper in a paper bag and dredge medallions in the mixture.

Heat a skillet until a drop of water sizzles away. Add canola oil and sauté medallions until lightly browned on each side. Serve medallions on a light layer of Cilantro-Cashew Pesto and garnish with minced mint leaves.

This dish goes well with Mesa Verde Green Bean and Pepper Salad, recipe on page 26.

| NUTRITIONAL FACTS PER SERVING | |
|---|---|
| Calories (kcal) | 267.2 |
| Cholesterol (mg) | 47 |
| Sodium (mg) | 41 |
| Total fat (g) | 21.9 |
| Saturated fat (g) | 5.2 |
| % Calories from fat | 74 |

*Servings*: 12

# Mesquite Chicken with Corn and Chile Dressing

❖

INGREDIENTS

8 chicken breast halves,
skinless and boned

3 drops liquid smoke

2 tablespoons lime juice

3 tablespoons canola oil

½ cup blue cornmeal

½ cup crumbled tortilla chips
(preferably blue corn)

½ cup diced green chiles

½ cup corn kernels

¼ cup diced pimiento

½ cup diced celery

¼ cup chopped cilantro

¼ cup chopped scallions

½ cup diced onion

1 cup Low-Salt Chicken Stock,
see recipe p. 51

½ cup Salsa Fresca,
see recipe p. 10

½ teaspoon oregano

½ teaspoon salt substitute

½ teaspoon pepper

Vegetable spray

½ cup Madeira

1 cup water

1 tablespoon Wondra flour

Pinch white pepper

METHOD

Wash chicken breasts, wipe dry, and place in deep bowl. Combine liquid smoke, lime juice, and canola oil to make a marinade. Pour over chicken and mix to coat. Cover and refrigerate while preparing dressing.

In a bowl, combine blue cornmeal, tortilla chips, chiles, corn, pimiento, celery, cilantro, scallions, onion, chicken broth, Salsa Fresca, oregano, salt, and pepper. Mix thoroughly.

Heat a large skillet until a drop of water sizzles away. Add chicken breasts and marinade. Lightly brown chicken on both sides. Set chicken aside, saving drippings for gravy.

❖

Preheat oven to 325 degrees F. Coat an 8-inch-square casserole dish with vegetable spray, add the dressing, and cover with aluminum foil. Bake for 30 minutes. Add chicken breasts on top of dressing and re-cover with foil, poking several holes in top of foil. Bake for 30 minutes. In the interim prepare gravy.

Add chicken drippings, Madeira, water, Wondra flour, and white pepper to saucepan. Bring to a low boil, stirring constantly, then reduce to simmer and cook until gravy starts to thicken.

Serve chicken breasts on a bed of dressing with a light layer of gravy over the top.

Notes: If you use mesquite-flavored chicken breasts, eliminate the liquid smoke flavoring.

Blue cornmeal and blue tortilla chips are available at most markets that sell organic produce and chemical-free meats. See "Mail Order Sources" at the back of the book.

Servings: 8

| NUTRITIONAL FACTS PER SERVING | |
| --- | --- |
| Calories (kcal) | 238.0 |
| Cholesterol (mg) | 62 |
| Sodium (mg) | 222 |
| Total fat (g) | 8.7 |
| Saturated fat (g) | 1.4 |
| % Calories from fat | 31 |

# Mole Poblano

## INGREDIENTS

3 cups Low-Salt Chicken Stock,
see recipe p. 51

4 chicken breast halves, skinless

4 chicken thighs, skinless

4 chicken drumsticks, skinless

1 tablespoon canola oil

3 dried ancho chiles,
seeded and chopped

3 fresh pasilla chiles,
seeded and chopped

2 fresh New Mexico chiles
(mild), seeded and chopped

1 clove garlic, minced

2 cups Salsa Mole,
see recipe p. 58

Sesame seeds for garnish

## METHOD

In a Dutch oven or deep skillet, bring chicken stock to a simmer. Add chicken breasts and legs. Cover and, turning occasionally, let simmer for 30 minutes or until chicken is done. Remove chicken from stock; reserve stock.

Heat a skillet until a drop of water quickly sizzles away. Add canola oil to coat skillet. Add ancho chiles, pasilla chiles, New Mexico chiles, and garlic. Fry until chiles are limp, then add reserved chicken stock. Bring to a boil and then reduce to simmer; cover and cook for 10 minutes. Remove from heat and bring to room temperature, then pour into a blender and purée to make a thin paste.

| NUTRITIONAL FACTS PER SERVING | |
| --- | --- |
| Calories (kcal) | 370.3 |
| Cholesterol (mg) | 119 |
| Sodium (mg) | 604 |
| Total fat (g) | 16.3 |
| Saturated fat (g) | 3.6 |
| % Calories from fat | 41 |

❖

Return chile purée to Dutch oven and bring to a simmer. Add chicken breasts and legs. Simmer chicken for 15 minutes. In the meantime, heat the Salsa Mole.

Serve the chicken with a nice covering of Salsa Mole and garnish with sesame seeds.

*Servings*: 4

# Pollo Escabache
## (Cold Pickled Chicken)

INGREDIENTS

¼ cup canola oil

4 chicken breast halves, skinless and boned

4 chicken thighs, skinless

8 chicken drumsticks, skinless

1 cup dry sherry

½ cup white vinegar

1 cup hot water

2 medium onions, quartered

2 carrots, sliced ¼-inch thick

1 small leek, sliced ¼-inch thick

1 teaspoon salt substitute

Bouquet garni of 1 celery top, 3 sprigs cilantro, bay leaf, 2 sprigs parsley, 1 star anise, ¼ teaspoon thyme tied in cheesecloth

2 lemons, sliced thin

2 limes, sliced thin

METHOD

In a Dutch oven, heat a drop of water until it quickly sizzles away. Add canola oil and spread to coat bottom of pan. Cut all chicken pieces in half. In batches, brown chicken on all sides and set aside. When all the chicken has been browned, add remaining ingredients (except lemon and lime) to the Dutch oven. Bring to a boil, reduce heat to simmer, and cook for 30 minutes or until chicken is tender. Remove from heat, discard bouquet, and, with a slotted spoon, remove chicken to a four- or five-quart casserole. Retain vegetables and sauce. Layer chicken pieces snugly in bottom of casserole. Pour vegetables and sauce over chicken. Decorate with slices of lime and lemon. Refrigerate for 5–6 hours or until mixture has jelled. Serve on chilled plates.

| NUTRITIONAL FACTS PER SERVING | |
| --- | --- |
| Calories (kcal) | 292.7 |
| Cholesterol (mg) | 95 |
| Sodium (mg) | 100 |
| Total fat (g) | 13.4 |
| Saturated fat (g) | 2.3 |
| % Calories from fat | 42 |

*Servings*: 8

# Pollo Escondido

❖

METHOD

Defat, rinse, and dry chicken breasts. In a small bowl, combine ground peppercorns, garlic powder, and masa flour and mix thoroughly. In another bowl, blend egg substitute and milk. Coat chicken breasts with egg-milk mixture and then dredge in flour mixture.

Heat a skillet until a drop of water sizzles away. Add olive oil and chicken breasts. Brown breasts on both sides. Add wine, reduce to a faint simmer, cover, and cook for 20 minutes; turn breasts over and cook for 10 more minutes.

Serve Pollo Escondido on a layer of Salsa Basil with additional salsa over the top.

*Servings*: 4

INGREDIENTS

4 chicken breast halves, skinless and boned

1 tablespoon peppercorns, freshly ground

1 teaspoon garlic powder

½ cup masa corn flour

⅛ cup egg substitute

¼ cup 1% milk

2 tablespoons olive oil

½ cup dry white wine

1 cup Salsa Basil, see recipe p. 56

| NUTRITIONAL FACTS PER SERVING | |
|---|---|
| Calories (kcal) | 313.1 |
| Cholesterol (mg) | 77 |
| Sodium (mg) | 112 |
| Total fat (g) | 12.5 |
| Saturated fat (g) | 2.6 |
| % Calories from fat | 36 |

# Pollo Naranja
## *(Orange-Flavored Chicken)*

INGREDIENTS

4 chicken breast halves,
skinless and boned

½ cup orange juice

¼ cup white wine

1 tablespoon achiote

1 tablespoon finely
chopped ginger

1 cup Mock Sour Cream, p. 53

¼ cup minced cilantro

¼ cup pomegranate seeds

METHOD

Place breasts bone side up in an
8-inch-square casserole dish.

In a blender, combine orange
juice, wine, and achiote and
blend. Pour into a skillet and
bring to a simmer. Then immediately remove from stove and let
cool. Pour mixture over chicken
breasts, cover with foil, and marinate for 30 minutes.

Preheat oven to 375 degrees F.

Remove foil from casserole dish.
Turn chicken breasts over and
sprinkle with chopped ginger.
Cover casserole dish with foil
and bake for 2 hours.

| NUTRITIONAL FACTS PER SERVING | |
| --- | --- |
| Calories (kcal) | 178.2 |
| Cholesterol (mg) | 70 |
| Sodium (mg) | 76 |
| Total fat (g) | 4.6 |
| Saturated fat (g) | 0.7 |
| % Calories from fat | 24 |

Remove chicken breasts to a pre-heated platter and cover with foil to keep warm. In a saucepan, combine marinade from casserole dish and Mock Sour Cream. Bring to a simmer and, stirring frequently, cook for 10 minutes. Ladle sauce over chicken breasts, garnish with cilantro and pomegranate seeds, and serve.

This chicken is also delicious served over rice.

*Servings*: 4

# Pork-Stuffed Brandied Turkey Medallions

INGREDIENTS

8 large turkey breast slices

3 scallions, minced

1 pound lean ground pork

½ cup minced pimiento

1 teaspoon coriander powder

1 teaspoon sage

½ teaspoon ground celery seed

Canola oil for frying

¼ cup brandy

1 cup evaporated skim milk

¼ cup orange juice

1 whole fresh pasilla chile,
seeded and chopped

1 teaspoon cornstarch

3 tablespoons water

Shredded zucchini to garnish

METHOD

Place a turkey breast slice between two pieces of wax paper and flatten it with a mallet, being careful not to break paper. The object is to have a very thin piece of meat. Repeat, using fresh wax paper for each breast. Set breasts aside.

In a large bowl, combine scallions, pork, pimiento, coriander, sage, and celery seed and form 8 rolls slightly shorter than the width of the turkey breasts.

At one edge of each turkey slice, place a roll of pork mix; roll up turkey breast, and seal with a toothpick.

Heat a Dutch oven until a drop of water quickly sizzles away.

| NUTRITIONAL FACTS PER SERVING | |
|---|---|
| Calories (kcal) | 332.1 |
| Cholesterol (mg) | 109 |
| Sodium (mg) | 184 |
| Total fat (g) | 13.5 |
| Saturated fat (g) | 3.9 |
| % Calories from fat | 34 |

Add canola oil to coat bottom of pan. Add turkey rolls and brown quickly on top and bottom. Reduce heat and cook for 5 minutes on one side and 2 minutes on the other.

Remove medallions to paper towel to drain. Spoon off cooking juices, being careful not to disturb drippings on bottom of pan. Return medallions to pan. Then add the brandy and flambé the medallions by tilting the pan slightly to the side and lighting the brandy with a match. Move medallions about in the flames. When the fire has burned itself out, remove medallions to a platter and cover with foil to keep warm.

Add evaporated skim milk, orange juice, and pasilla chile to drippings in Dutch oven; deglaze and bring to a simmer. In a small vessel, mix cornstarch and water to form a thin white paste. Add to sauce in Dutch oven and stir in. Let sauce simmer for 2 more minutes, then remove from heat.

Serve medallions with a coat of brandy-orange sauce and top with shredded zucchini.

Note: It's better to have your butcher slice an uncooked turkey breast for you rather than to rely on the packaged slices.

Servings: 8

# Pork Tamales

## INGREDIENTS

3 tablespoons canola oil

½ cup slivered almonds

1 medium onion, chopped

½ cup diced green chiles

½ cup diced red bell pepper

1 tablespoon chili powder

¼ teaspoon cayenne

1 teaspoon coriander powder

2 cups diced,
cooked pork shoulder

1 cup red wine

Corn husks for 24 tamales
(about 35–40)

5 cups Masa Dough for Beef or
Pork Tamales, see recipe p. 133

Green taco sauce

## METHOD

Heat a skillet until a drop of water quickly sizzles away. Add canola oil to coat skillet. Brown almond slivers, then add onion, green chiles, bell pepper, chili powder, cayenne, and coriander and sauté until onion is limp. Add pork and wine and simmer for 10 minutes or until most of the liquid is cooked off. Remove from heat and bring to room temperature.

Soak corn husks in water for at least 15 minutes before using (they will become almost soft). Lay out 1 husk or 2 slightly over-lapped, so that the width of available husk is 6 to 8 inches, with pointed ends away from

| NUTRITIONAL FACTS PER SERVING | |
|---|---|
| Calories (kcal) | 324.9 |
| Cholesterol (mg) | 17 |
| Sodium (mg) | 106 |
| Total fat (g) | 20.8 |
| Saturated fat (g) | 2.3 |
| % Calories from fat | 56 |

and wide ends near you. Starting at the right edge, spread 3 table-spoons of masa dough across husk, leaving 1 inch of husk at left and 1½–2 inches at top and bottom. Spoon a couple of tablespoons of filling onto masa; then, starting from the right, fold husk to just beyond the middle. Fold left side of husk over top of right. Fold bottom of husk to just short of the middle and the top of husk over the top of the bottom fold. Bind filled tamale with strips of soaked corn husks. Continue until all tamales are completed. Yield should be between 20 and 24, according to how much filling you use in each.

In a clam steamer or spaghetti pot, add enough water to come just below the removable inner shell. Lay tamales folded side down on bottom of shell and continue to stack until all tamales are evenly distributed, leaving plenty of room for steam to circulate. Steam for 45 minutes to an hour. Masa dough should be firm and not stick to husk when removed.

Serve with green taco sauce.

*Servings:* 10–12

# Quail Breasts with Cilantro Salsa

INGREDIENTS

½ teaspoon chili powder

¼ cup lime juice

½ cup light beer

16 quail breasts, skinless

2 cups croutons, crushed

¼ cup all-purpose flour

¼ cup canola oil

1 cup Cilantro Salsa,
see recipe p. 46

METHOD

In a deep bowl, blend chili powder, lime juice, and beer. Add quail breasts; marinate in refrigerator for 2 hours.

After 2 hours, mix crushed croutons and flour in another bowl. Roll out a couple of pieces of wax paper on a flat surface. Remove a quail breast from marinade and dredge in flour mixture. Place floured quail breast on wax paper. Repeat until all quail breasts are floured, leaving plenty of space between breasts.

Heat a skillet until a drop of water sizzles away. Reduce heat to medium and add canola oil. Brown breasts three at a time on both sides. Remove breasts to a heated platter and cover with foil to keep warm until all are done. Serve with Cilantro Salsa.

| NUTRITIONAL FACTS PER SERVING | |
|---|---|
| Calories (kcal) | 566.7 |
| Cholesterol (mg) | 130 |
| Sodium (mg) | 253 |
| Total fat (g) | 27.6 |
| Saturated fat (g) | 3.6 |
| % Calories from fat | 45 |

*Servings:* 4

# Sea Bass Flamenco

4 ¼-pound sea bass steaks

2 tablespoons olive oil

1 dried serrano chile, crumbled

3 cloves garlic, minced

1 teaspoon lemon zest

1 tablespoon achiote

1 teaspoon unsweetened chocolate

1 cup white wine

METHOD

Wash fish and pat dry. Heat a skillet until a drop of water quickly sizzles away. Add olive oil to coat skillet. Add sea bass steaks and cook for 2 minutes on each side. Remove steaks to platter and cover with foil to keep warm. Reduce heat to simmer.

To the skillet, add serrano chile, garlic, lemon zest, achiote, chocolate, and white wine. Bring to a simmer and, stirring constantly, cook until chocolate is dissolved and mixture is reduced slightly.

Pour sauce over sea bass fillets and serve.

*Servings:* 4

| NUTRITIONAL FACTS PER SERVING | |
| --- | --- |
| Calories (kcal) | 218.3 |
| Cholesterol (mg) | 47 |
| Sodium (mg) | 187 |
| Total fat (g) | 9.3 |
| Saturated fat (g) | 1.2 |
| % Calories from fat | 39 |

# Sirloin Tip Fajitas

INGREDIENTS

1½ pounds sirloin tip

½ cup Fajita Marinade,
see recipe p. 49

Canola oil for frying

1 medium onion, sliced in rings

1 green bell pepper,
sliced in rings

1 red bell pepper, sliced in rings

8 large low-fat flour tortillas

Green taco sauce to taste

METHOD

Slice sirloin tip in ¼-inch strips against the grain. Put meat in a glass or ceramic bowl and cover with Marinade. Let set 1–2 hours.

Heat a large iron skillet until a drop of water quickly sizzles away. Add canola oil to coat skillet. Fry onion and bell peppers until limp. Store in foil to keep warm. Add meat to pan and cook until lightly brown.

To serve, place equal portions of meat, onions, and peppers in center of a tortilla. Add green taco sauce. Repeat process with remaining tortillas. Fajitas can be eaten in-hand or served on a plate.

| NUTRITIONAL FACTS PER SERVING | |
| --- | --- |
| Calories (kcal) | 281.6 |
| Cholesterol (mg) | 48 |
| Sodium (mg) | 268 |
| Total fat (g) | 11.3 |
| Saturated fat (g) | 2.7 |
| % Calories from fat | 37 |

Pictured: *Sirloin Tip Fajitas*.

*Servings*: 8

# Truchas Nuevo Mexico
## *(New Mexico Trout)*

INGREDIENTS

4 trout fillets, boned

1 cup finely chopped onion

Dash black pepper

2 fresh mint sprigs

Dash thyme

2 fresh rosemary sprigs

1 bay leaf

1 cup red wine

2 tablespoons olive oil

¼ cup egg substitute

¼ teaspoon salt substitute

¼ cup minced black olives

¼ cup diced pimiento

METHOD

Clean trout fillets in cold water. In a ceramic or glass casserole, place the trout, leaving space between them. Spread onion evenly over trout. In a mortar, combine black pepper, mint, thyme, rosemary, and bay leaf; crush to release flavors, and sprinkle over trout in casserole. Pour wine over all, cover with plastic wrap, and marinate for 1 hour.

Remove trout from marinade, reserving marinade. Bring a skillet to medium heat and add olive oil to coat pan. Cook trout 2 minutes on each side, then remove to a warm plate and cover with foil. Add marinade to skillet to make a broth. Bring

| NUTRITIONAL FACTS PER SERVING | |
| --- | --- |
| Calories (kcal) | 240.1 |
| Cholesterol (mg) | 45 |
| Sodium (mg) | 184 |
| Total fat (g) | 11.3 |
| Saturated fat (g) | 1.7 |
| % Calories from fat | 37 |

to a boil, then reduce to simmer and cook 10 minutes. Strain broth into a deep bowl. Mix ½ cup of broth with egg substitute. Return remainder of broth to skillet and add broth-egg blend and salt. Simmer for 2–3 minutes.

To serve, pour broth over trout and garnish with black olives and pimiento.

*Servings:* 4

# Venison Caliente

2 dried serrano chiles,
minced with seeds

½ teaspoon black pepper

½ teaspoon sage

½ teaspoon curry powder

½ teaspoon dill seed

2 cloves garlic, minced

½ cup minced green chiles

¼ cup chopped cilantro

3 tablespoons apricot jam

2 tablespoons Worcestershire
sauce

8 ¼-pound venison steaks

5 tablespoons olive oil

½ cup chopped white onions

½ cup minced celery

½ cup minced carrots

1 cup dry white wine

½ cup Mock Sour Cream,
see recipe p. 53

½ cup crumbled croutons

METHOD

Prepare your barbecue grill. In a mortar, combine dried serrano chiles, black pepper, sage, curry powder, and dill seed. Crush to blend spices. In a mixing bowl, add garlic, green chiles, cilantro, apricot jam, Worcestershire sauce, and spice mix from the mortar. Stir to form a paste. Remove one-third of mixture and set aside.

On a cutting board, flatten each venison steak with a mallet until it is about ¼ inch thick. Coat top of each steak with the paste. Roll steaks and secure each with a toothpick or skewer.

With a basting brush, paint a barbecue grill with 2 tablespoons of olive oil to keep steaks from sticking. Place steaks on grill and brown evenly on all sides, about 5 minutes between turns.

Heat a saucepan until a drop of water sizzles away. Add remaining 3 tablespoons of olive oil and sauté onions, celery, and carrots. Add wine, sour cream, croutons, and the reserved paste mixture; blend to mix and bring to a simmer. Stir until mixture starts to thicken into a sauce. Serve venison covered with the sauce.

Thin-sliced beef sirloin steaks make a good substitute for the venison. For more intense chile flavor, make the paste ahead of time and marinate the steaks in it for an hour or two.

*Servings*: 8

| NUTRITIONAL FACTS PER SERVING | |
|---|---|
| Calories (kcal) | 269.1 |
| Cholesterol (mg) | 94 |
| Sodium (mg) | 289 |
| Total fat (g) | 10.7 |
| Saturated fat (g) | 2.0 |
| % Calories from fat | 36 |

*Pictured on following page* : Hopi Fry Bread (*see recipe* p. 131) *and Colorful Jalapeño Cornbread* (p. 130).

❖ ❖ ❖

# Breads,
# Masa,
# and Pasta

# Colorful Jalapeño Cornbread

❖

## INGREDIENTS

2 cups 1% milk

½ cup egg substitute

2 jalapeño peppers

2 cups masa harina (corn flour)

1 cup all-purpose flour

3 tablespoons turbinado sugar

2 tablespoons baking powder

½ cup minced red bell pepper

½ cup diced green chiles

½ cup minced onion

½ cup canola oil

Vegetable spray

## METHOD

Preheat oven to 400 degrees F.

Combine milk, egg substitute, and jalapeños in a blender and blend for 25–30 seconds to finely grind ingredients.

In a large mixing bowl, combine masa harina, flour, sugar, baking powder, red bell pepper, green chiles, and onion. Blend well, slowly adding the canola oil. When thoroughly mixed, add mixture from blender and stir until thoroughly blended.

Spray a muffin tin with vegetable spray. Spoon cornbread mixture about three-fourths full in each cupped section.

Bake for 25 minutes. Remove and let cool.

*Servings:* 16

| NUTRITIONAL FACTS PER SERVING | |
| --- | --- |
| Calories (kcal) | 159.6 |
| Cholesterol (mg) | 2 |
| Sodium (mg) | 163 |
| Total fat (g) | 7.2 |
| Saturated fat (g) | 0.7 |
| % Calories from fat | 40 |

# Hopi Fry Bread

❖

## METHOD

In a deep bowl, combine flour, powdered milk, baking powder, and salt substitute. Add warm water and mix to form a soft dough. Knead until dough is satiny and springy. Make into 12 balls. Brush top of each ball with canola oil. Cover with a damp cloth and let set for 45 minutes.

Lightly flour a bread board or smooth counter top and roll out each ball to a 4-inch circle. With your hands, stretch each circle to a diameter of 7–8 inches. Poke a hole in center of each piece and then fry in canola oil over moderate heat until lightly browned, turning once. Drain on paper towels.

Serve with honey or a dusting of powdered sugar.

*Servings*: 12

## INGREDIENTS

2 cups all-purpose flour

⅓ cup powdered nonfat milk

2 teaspoons baking powder

1 teaspoon salt substitute

¾ cup warm water

Canola oil for brushing on dough and for frying

| NUTRITIONAL FACTS PER SERVING | |
|---|---|
| Calories (kcal) | 105.9 |
| Cholesterol (mg) | 0 |
| Sodium (mg) | 53 |
| Total fat (g) | 3.3 |
| Saturated fat (g) | 0.3 |
| % Calories from fat | 29 |

# Croutons Mi Casa

### INGREDIENTS

2 slices bread

⅛ teaspoon thyme

⅛ teaspoon oregano

⅛ teaspoon garlic powder

⅛ teaspoon sage

⅛ teaspoon basil

Dash cayenne

1 teaspoon canola oil

### METHOD

Cut bread in ½-inch cubes. Discard crusts. Let bread cubes set out until they start to harden; turn over and let other side start to harden.

Combine thyme, oregano, garlic, sage, basil, and cayenne in a mortar and grind to blend spices.

In a skillet, heat a drop of water until it sizzles away, then add canola oil and spread around bottom. Add bread cubes and spread evenly across skillet, preferably in a single layer. Heat bread cubes until firm and slightly browned. Put bread cubes in a large bowl, sprinkle spice mix over them, and toss to coat.

Refrigerate in an airtight container or use immediately to accompany Caesar's Salad El Paso (p. 16) or other salad recipes.

*Servings: Makes about ¾–1 cup*

| NUTRITIONAL FACTS PER SERVING | |
| --- | --- |
| Calories (kcal) | 17.7 |
| Cholesterol (mg) | 0 |
| Sodium (mg) | 27 |
| Total fat (g) | 0.6 |
| Saturated fat (g) | 0.1 |
| % Calories from fat | 32 |

# Masa Dough for Beef or Pork Tamales

**METHOD**

In a large bowl, combine masa, white cornmeal, and baking powder and blend. Make a well in the center of the flour. Pour the canola oil into the well and mix to absorb. Dissolve the achiote in the water. Add dissolved paste, turmeric, chicken stock, and egg substitute to the masa mixture. Work masa dough with your hands until it holds together without crumbling (add more stock ¼ cup at a time if needed).

Cover with a damp cloth and refrigerate until needed; dough will keep as long as a week.

Masa dough can also be used to make tortillas and sopaipillas.

*Servings: Makes enough for about 40 tamales*

**INGREDIENTS**

2 cups masa harina

2 cups white cornmeal

1 tablespoon baking powder

1 cup canola oil

1 tablespoon achiote

½ cup water

½ teaspoon turmeric

3 cups Low-Salt Chicken Stock, see recipe p. 51

½ cup egg substitute

| NUTRITIONAL FACTS PER SERVING | |
|---|---:|
| Calories (kcal) | 95.9 |
| Cholesterol (mg) | 0 |
| Sodium (mg) | 33 |
| Total fat (g) | 6.0 |
| Saturated fat (g) | 0.5 |
| % Calories from fat | 56 |

# Lorenzo's Tex-Mex Lasagna

INGREDIENTS

2 tablespoons canola oil

1½ pounds lean ground beef, chili grind preferred

½ teaspoon oregano

2 teaspoons cumin

1 tablespoon paprika

1 tablespoon chili powder

¼ teaspoon garlic powder

1 teaspoon salt substitute

½ teaspoon black pepper

1½ cups diced green chiles

3 cups diced tomatoes

Vegetable spray

10 corn tortillas

2 cups low-fat cottage cheese, drained

1 cup shredded skim-milk mozzarella

2 tablespoons egg substitute

1 cup shredded low-sodium cheddar cheese

2 cups shredded romaine lettuce

½ cup diced pimientos

METHOD

Heat a skillet until a drop of water quickly sizzles away. Add canola oil to coat skillet. Add beef and brown; drain on paper towels.

In a large bowl, combine oregano, cumin, paprika, chili powder, garlic powder, salt sub-stitute, and black pepper. Add drained beef, chiles, and to-matoes; stir to mix. Spray a large shallow casserole dish with vege-table spray. Line sides and  bottom with tortillas. Spread beef-spice mixture on tortillas. Lay more tortillas over beef mixture.

Preheat oven to 375 degrees F.

In a bowl, combine cottage cheese, mozzarella, and egg substitute; ladle mixture over tortillas. Cover casserole with foil and bake for 30 minutes.

In a mixing bowl, combine cheddar cheese, lettuce, and

pimientos. Sprinkle mixture over casserole and serve.

*Servings*: 8

| NUTRITIONAL FACTS PER SERVING | |
| --- | --- |
| Calories (kcal) | 466.7 |
| Cholesterol (mg) | 79 |
| Sodium (mg) | 681 |
| Total fat (g) | 23.4 |
| Saturated fat (g) | 9.1 |
| % Calories from fat | 42 |

# Salsa Basil con Pasta

INGREDIENTS

2 cups pasta shells,
prepared al dente

1 cup Salsa Basil,
see recipe p. 56

½ cup shredded queso anejo
(a Mexican hard cheese)

METHOD

While pasta is cooking, heat
Salsa Basil; then pour the sauce
over pasta shells and mix thoroughly. Sprinkle with queso
anejo and serve.

Salsa Basil con Pasta makes a
great main dish accompanied by
Caesar's Salad El Paso, p. 16.

*Serving:* 8

| NUTRITIONAL FACTS PER SERVING | |
| --- | --- |
| Calories (kcal) | 97.6 |
| Cholesterol (mg) | 11 |
| Sodium (mg) | 78 |
| Total fat (g) | 4.8 |
| Saturated fat (g) | 2.3 |
| % Calories from fat | 44 |

*Pictured: Noodles Grande with Shrimp and
Red Bell Peppers (see recipe p. 138).*

# Noodles Grande with
# Shrimp and Red Bell Peppers

## INGREDIENTS

16 lasagna noodles

Vegetable spray

1½ cups Low-Salt Chicken Stock,
see recipe p. 51

¼ pound shrimp,
shelled and deveined

2 stalks celery, minced

1 red bell pepper, minced

1 fresh pasilla chile,
seeded and deveined

4 tablespoons egg substitute

½ cup seasoned bread crumbs

¼ teaspoon oregano

1 tablespoon tomato paste

½ cup dry white wine

¼ cup evaporated skim milk

Dash nutmeg

## METHOD

Prepare lasagna noodles as directed on package, only do not use salt. Spray a long sheet of wax paper with vegetable spray. Drain noodles and lay them separately on wax paper.

Place chicken stock in a pot and bring to a simmer. Add shrimp and cook for 1 minute  or until they turn pink. Remove shrimp with a slotted spoon, reserving stock.

In a glass bowl, combine shrimp, celery, and red bell pepper. Slice pasilla chile in julienne strips and add to shrimp mix. Add egg substitute, bread crumbs, and oregano and blend in.

Spray top side of lasagna noodles with vegetable oil. Using a wine glass, roll a noodle on the narrow end to form a tube a couple of inches high. Secure noodle with a toothpick. Continue until all noodles are rolled. Place noodle tubes upright in bottom of shallow casserole dish. They should fill the bottom.

Spoon equal portions of shrimp-pepper mix into center of each noodle tube. In a bowl, combine reserved stock, tomato paste, dry white wine, evaporated skim milk, and nutmeg and blend.

Preheat oven to 350 degrees F.

Using a funnel, pour wine sauce around the outside of the noodles. Spray tops of lasagna tubes with vegetable oil. Cover with foil and bake for 30 minutes.

When sliding a spatula under the tubes to serve them, be careful that their contents don't fall out. Serve with a spoonful or two of cooking sauce.

*Servings*: 8

| NUTRITIONAL FACTS PER SERVING | |
|---|---|
| Calories (kcal) | 250.0 |
| Cholesterol (mg) | 22 |
| Sodium (mg) | 367 |
| Total fat (g) | 4.6 |
| Saturated fat (g) | 0.2 |
| % Calories from fat | 16 |

# Sopaipillas

❖

### INGREDIENTS

4 cups all-purpose flour, sifted

1½ teaspoons salt substitute

1 tablespoon baking powder

2 tablespoons canola oil

½ cup warm water,
about 110 degrees F.

1¼ cups 1% milk, scalded
and at room temperature

Canola oil for frying

### METHOD

Combine sifted flour, salt substitute, and baking powder and mix. Combine canola oil, water, and milk and add to flour mixture in ½-cup increments, working dough into a springy ball. Knead dough 10–15 times, then cover with a bowl and set aside for 15–20 minutes.

Divide dough into four equal parts, roll each to a ¼-inch thickness, and cut in triangles or squares.

Heat a skillet until a drop of water quickly sizzles away. Add canola oil and fry sopaipillas, a few at a time, until golden brown and puffy. Drain on paper towels and serve as bread or dessert rolls.

*Servings: Makes about 48 small portions*

| NUTRITIONAL FACTS PER SERVING | |
| --- | --- |
| Calories (kcal) | 54.8 |
| Cholesterol (mg) | 0 |
| Sodium (mg) | 20 |
| Total fat (g) | 1.7 |
| Saturated fat (g) | 0.2 |
| % Calories from fat | 29 |

# Spicy Triple Noodle Casserole

### METHOD

Prepare noodles as directed on package, substituting chicken stock for water and omitting salt. When cooked, drain noodles and pour into a bowl, reserving cooking stock.

Bring cooking stock to a simmer. Add shallots, tomatoes, green chiles, jalapeño, and corn; cook until most of the liquid has evaporated and sauce is starting to thicken.

Preheat oven to 350 degrees F.

Spray a 1½-quart casserole with vegetable spray. Lay noodles in casserole to form a base. Spoon stock-vegetable mixture over noodles, sprinkle with cheese, cover with foil, and bake for 30 minutes.

*Servings: 8*

### INGREDIENTS

3 ounces spinach egg noodles

3 ounces plain egg noodles

3 ounces carrot egg noodles

2 cups Low-Salt Chicken Stock, see recipe p. 51

3 shallots, minced

4 Roma tomatoes, seeded and chopped

½ cup diced green chiles

1 jalapeño pepper, minced

¼ cup fresh corn kernels

Vegetable spray

½ cup shredded low-sodium colby cheese

| NUTRITIONAL FACTS PER SERVING | |
|---|---|
| Calories (kcal) | 119.1 |
| Cholesterol (mg) | 21 |
| Sodium (mg) | 96 |
| Total fat (g) | 1.7 |
| Saturated fat (g) | 0.5 |
| % Calories from fat | 13 |

*Pictured on following page: Orange-Rice Pudding (see recipe p. 144) and Strawberries Vegas (p. 145).*

❖ ❖ ❖

# Desserts

# Orange-Rice Pudding

❖

## INGREDIENTS

4 cups cooked rice

¼ cup raisins

2 tablespoons orange zest

½ cup egg substitute

3 cups 1% milk

½ cup turbinado sugar

Dash allspice

1 teaspoon vanilla extract

¼ cup water

1 package unsweetened gelatin powder

Orange slices to garnish

## METHOD

In a deep ceramic bowl, combine rice, raisins, and orange zest. In a saucepan, combine egg substitute, milk, sugar, allspice, and vanilla extract; bring to a simmer, then add to rice mix.

To a small bowl, add the water and sprinkle the gelatin powder on top. Let stand 2 minutes, until powder is softened.

Combine gelatin with rice mixture. Stir to blend well. Spoon into serving dishes. Cover and chill in refrigerator.

Garnish with orange slices to serve.

| NUTRITIONAL FACTS PER SERVING | |
| --- | --- |
| Calories (kcal) | 230.9 |
| Cholesterol (mg) | 4 |
| Sodium (mg) | 85 |
| Total fat (g) | 1.7 |
| Saturated fat (g) | 0.8 |
| % Calories from fat | 7 |

*Servings:* 8

# Strawberries Vegas

INGREDIENTS

2 cups fresh strawberries, cleaned

¼ teaspoon mace

2 tablespoons honey

½ cup plain low-fat yogurt

1 cup mandarin oranges

METHOD

Cut strawberries in half lengthwise. Put half of strawberries in a blender. Add mace, honey, yogurt, and ½ cup of oranges and purée. Spoon purée into individual dessert cups. Put in freezer for 20 minutes to chill.

To serve, top with remaining strawberry halves and mandarin oranges.

*Serving*: 4

| NUTRITIONAL FACTS PER SERVING | |
|---|---|
| Calories (kcal) | 89.6 |
| Cholesterol (mg) | 2 |
| Sodium (mg) | 23 |
| Total fat (g) | 0.6 |
| Saturated fat (g) | 0.3 |
| % Calories from fat | 6 |

# Capirotada with Yogurt
## (Mexican-Style Bread Pudding)

INGREDIENTS

8 bolillos (Mexican hard rolls)

¼ cup canola oil

2 cups turbinado sugar

2 cups water

1 cup plain low-fat yogurt

½ cup orange juice

½ teaspoon nutmeg

Vegetable spray

Shredded jack cheese to garnish

METHOD

Cut each roll lengthwise in four slices. Heat a skillet until a drop of water quickly sizzles away. Add canola oil and fry bread on both sides. Remove to paper towels to drain.

In a saucepan, combine sugar, water, yogurt, orange juice, and nutmeg; boil until sugar dissolves and liquid is the consistency of honey.

Preheat oven to 300 degrees F.

Spray a large shallow casserole dish with vegetable spray. Cover bottom with bread slices. Pour sugar liquid over the top. Bake for 15 minutes. Remove from oven. Sprinkle with cheese and let cool before serving.

*Servings: 8*

| NUTRITIONAL FACTS PER SERVING | |
|---|---|
| Calories (kcal) | 450.9 |
| Cholesterol (mg) | 3 |
| Sodium (mg) | 331 |
| Total fat (g) | 10.2 |
| Saturated fat (g) | 1.4 |
| % Calories from fat | 20 |

# Dulce de Piñon y Pacana

*(Pecan and Pine Nut Dessert)*

INGREDIENTS

2 cups 1% milk

¾ cup roasted pine nuts (piñons)

¾ cup pecans (or walnuts)

½ cup egg substitute

¼ cup granulated sugar

¼ teaspoon nutmeg

1 tablespoon masa harina

1 cup Strawberry-Vanilla Sauce, see recipe p. 150

Pecans (or walnuts) and pine nut to garnish

METHOD

In a blender, combine half of the milk, the pine nuts, and the pecans and purée. Add remaining milk and egg substitute and blend.

In a skillet, cook over low heat, stirring constantly until mixture starts to thicken. Add sugar, nutmeg, and masa harina and continue to stir until thick.

Let cool. Serve in dessert cups. Drizzle desserts with Strawberry-Vanilla Sauce and sprinkle with whole pecans and pine nuts.

*Note:* Dulce de Pinon y Pacana is very rich—a little taste goes a long way.

*Servings:* 8

| NUTRITIONAL FACTS PER SERVING | |
|---|---|
| Calories (kcal) | 217.0 |
| Cholesterol (mg) | 3 |
| Sodium (mg) | 83 |
| Total fat (g) | 13.1 |
| Saturated fat (g) | 1.5 |
| % Calories from fat | 51 |

# Sofia's Chile Jelly Buñuelos

INGREDIENTS

8 Sopaipillas, see recipe p. 140

1 cup jalapeño jelly

1 cup Mock Sour Cream,
see recipe p. 53

Pecans or walnuts

METHOD

Into center of each sopaipilla, spoon a tablespoon of jelly. Top with a tablespoon of Mock Sour Cream, garnish with pecans, and serve.

*Servings:* 8

| NUTRITIONAL FACTS PER SERVING | |
|---|---|
| Calories (kcal) | 164.9 |
| Cholesterol (mg) | 1 |
| Sodium (mg) | 78 |
| Total fat (g) | 1.9 |
| Saturated fat (g) | 0.3 |
| % Calories from fat | 10 |

*Pictured: Sophia's Chile Jelly Buñuelos.*

# Strawberry-Vanilla Sauce

❖

## INGREDIENTS

2 tablespoons 1% milk

3 tablespoons egg substitute

2 tablespoons turbinado sugar

1 teaspoon cornstarch

¾ cup evaporated skim milk

½ cup strawberry jelly

1 teaspoon vanilla extract

## METHOD

Combine milk, egg substitute, sugar, and cornstarch in a saucepan. Bring heat up slowly, stirring constantly. Slowly add evaporated milk, continuing to stir. Add strawberry jelly and blend in. Add vanilla and immediately remove from heat and let cool before using.

*Servings: Makes about 1½ cups (about 3 servings)*

| NUTRITIONAL FACTS PER SERVING | |
| --- | --- |
| Calories (kcal) | 51.2 |
| Cholesterol (mg) | 1 |
| Sodium (mg) | 50 |
| Total fat (g) | 0.3 |
| Saturated fat (g) | 0.1 |
| % Calories from fat | 5 |

# Mail-Order Sources

SESPE CREEK SPICE AND CHILI COMPANY

929 Blaine Avenue

Fillmore, CA 93015

(805) 524-2078

fax (805) 388-9593

chili powders, cumin, oregano, other spices


HATCH CHILE COMPANY

2833 Rhode Island, NE

Albuquerque, NM 87111

(800) 933-2736

canned chile, other food products, etc.


SANTA CRUZ CHILI AND SPICE COMPANY

P.O. Box 177

Tumacacori, AZ 85640

(602) 398-2591

chile spices fresh, dried, powdered


LOS ARCOS TORTILLAS

1705 Stocker Street

No. Las Vegas, NV 89030

(702) 399-3300

tortillas, masa, Mexican spices,

achiote, chiles, canned products

# Acknowledgments

❖

I have to express my most sincere thanks to my runnin' mate, Jodi. She spent countless hours editing various versions of the manuscript and suffering through my trial runs on the recipes. She's a good hand and a great wife. There ain't none better than Jod.

I have to make a confession. Unknown to Jodi, the salt shaker she loves to use has contained a salt substitute for several months. I hope this doesn't come as a shock, dear.

The people at Northland Publishing are miracle workers. If I needed something, they found it. If I was lost for words, they corralled some. When I was worried about fat grams, sodium count, or calories, they rounded up a top-drawer registered dietician. When I needed a place to prep food, they provided a kitchen. A tip of the Stetson to these folks.

Special thanks goes to Jill Mason in Austin, Texas, who hired on to edit the manuscript and scratch at my errors. She has a good eye and made the final product sparkle.

Registered dietitian Stephen Sapienza fine-tuned the nutritional facts and brought to light those recipes that best suit a balanced low-salt, low-fat diet. He's a professional, and when he recommends a recipe, he knows what he's doing.

The dazzling photography comes from the talents of Owen Lowe of Owen Lowe Photography in Flagstaff, Arizona, and Trina Stahl and Rudy Ramos from Northland's art department. It took five days of food preparation and camera work to create the final product. It was a haul. In the interim, Owen, Trina, and Rudy ate well, to say the least. I can't forget Bob and Lisa Brownfield, who provided their kitchen and garage for nearly a week.

Thanks also to Robert D. Forsyth, M.D., who unknowingly blazed the trail. His interest in my health made it all happen.

Finally, I give a nod to my Wyoming cowboy buddy Don "Dutch" Grace, who kept up the encouragement and, at times, washed the dishes and helped prepare the recipes. He now considers himself an aficionado of southwestern cooking.

The recipes and most nutritional facts in this book were created on an IBM-style personal computer using MasterCook II for Windows (Arion Software, Austin, Texas, copyright © 1993).

Additional reference was provided by The Complete Book of Food Counts, by Corinne T. Netzer (Dell Publishing, New York, New York, copyright © 1988).

# Index

American Dietetic Association, viii

American Heart Association, viii, ix

Ancho Chile Sauce, 41, 86

Arbol chiles, 44


Basil, 56

Basque-Style Stuffed Peppers, 82-84

Bean, Corn, and Squash Caldo, 33

Beans

    black, xii, 3, 66, 72

    green, 26

    lima, 65

    pinto, 33, 65, 70

    red, 80

Beef, 34, 37, 50, 78, 98-99, 134-135

Beer, 48, 82, 96, 104, 120

Bell peppers, 19, 26, 71, 82-84, 138-139

Bisque, 28, 30-31

Black Bean Dip, 3

Black Bean Frijoles, 3, 66, 72

    comparison of traditional and

        modified, xii

Brandy, 116-117

Bread pudding, 146

Buñuelos, 148

Burritos, 67, 72-73

Butter lettuce, 19


Cactus, 60

Caesar's Salad El Paso, 16

Canola oil, x, xi

Capirotada with Yogurt, 146

Carrots, 20, 69

Cashews, 47

Catfish Jambalaya, 85

Center for Science in the

    Public Interest, viii, xi

Cheddar cheese, 96-97, 134-135

Cheese. See Cheddar cheese,

    Colby cheese, Cottage cheese,

    Cream cheese, Mozzarella cheese,

    Neufchâtel cheese, Queso anejo

Cheese and Egg Burrito, 67

Chicken, 24, 42, 51, 86-88, 90-91,

    92-93, 108-109, 112, 113, 114-115

Chicken Enchiladas, 86-88

Chicken Filling, 42

Chicken Ole! Ole!, 90-91

Chicken Santa Fe with Tomato

    Chile Gravy, 40, 92-93

Chile chimayo, 45

Chile Dill Sauce, 43, 106

Chile Elk Steaks, 94-95

Chile-Garlic Vinegar, 44

Chile serrano, 44

Chile Verde Roberto, 89

Chile, Radish, and Queso Dip, 4

Chiles, xii-xiv, 4, 5, 6-7, 23, 40, 41, 43,

    44, 45, 54, 55, 60, 110

    mail-order sauces, 151

Chili, 34-36, 89

Chilled Tomato and Cottage Cheese Soup, 32

Chimayo Chile Salad Dressing, 45

Cholesterol, viii-ix

Cilantro, 10, 46, 47

Cilantro-Cashew Pesto, 47, 107

Cilantro Salsa, 46, 120

Colby cheese, 141

Cold Pickled Chicken, 112

Colorful Jalapeño Cornbread, 130

Corn and Chile Dressing, 108-109

Corn, 28, 33

Corn Bisque, 28

Cornbread, 130

Cottage cheese, 4, 5, 32, 43, 53, 134-135

Crab, 18

Crab and Jicama Salad, 18

Cream cheese, xi, 92

Creole rice and red beans, 80

Croutons Mi Casa, 132

Dill, 43

Dressings, 20, 22, 45, 61, 108-109

Drunken Porker Enchiladas, 96-97

Drunken Porker Filling, 48, 96

Dulce de Piñon y Pacana, 147

Egg substitute, xi-xii, 67, 150

Elk, 94-95

Enchiladas, 86-88
    sauce, 55, 72, 73, 78

Fajita Marinade, 49, 122

Fajitas, 122

Fat, viii-ix, xi

Fillet Brochettes, 98-99

Fish, 11, 52, 74-75, 85, 101-102, 106,
    121, 124-125

Five Pepper Salad, 19

Garlic, 44

Golden Lamb Chops, 100

Graham crackers, 12

Gravy, 40

Green beans, 26

Green chiles, 40, 43, 46, 48, 60, 76,
    89, 94, 108, 134

Green chili, 89

Grilled Chicken and Zucchini Salad, 24

Hacienda Hash Browns, 68

Ham, 70

Herbed Chile Dip, 5

Hopi Fry Bread, 131

Huachinango San Felipe, 106

Huachinango Vera Cruz, 101-102

Jalapeño peppers, 60, 104, 130
    jelly, 148

Japon chiles, 44

Javelina Brochettes with Salsa
    Tequila, 60, 104-105

Jerky, 14

Jicama, 18, 20

Jicama-Carrot-Onion Salad, 20

Lamb, 47, 100, 107

Lamb Medallions with Cilantro-Cashew
    Pesto, 47, 107

Lasagna, 134-135, 138-139

Lettuce, 16, 18, 19, 20, 22

Lima and Pinto Beans, 65

Lime juice, 8, 11

Lorenzo's Tex-Mex Lasagna, 134-135

Low-fat cooking, viii-ix, x-xiv

Low-Salt Beef Stock, 50

Low-Salt Chicken Stock, 51, 56, 82,
    89, 92, 108, 110, 133, 141

Low-Salt Fish Stock, 52, 101

Low-sodium cooking, viii-ix, x-xiv

Marinade, 49

Masa Dough for Beef or Pork Tamales,
118, 133

Mesa Verde Green Bean and Pepper Salad,
26, 107

Mesquite Chicken with Corn and
Chile Dressing, 108-109

Mexican-Style Bread Pudding, 146

Mock Sour Cream, xii, 6, 7, 53,
61, 86, 148

Mole, 58-59

Mole Poblano, 110-111

Mozzarella cheese, 67, 134-135


Neufchâtel cheese, xi, 4, 5, 6, 8, 77

New Mexico Trout, 124-125

Noodles Grande with Shrimp and
Red Bell Peppers, 138-139

Nopalito, 60

Nutritional analysis, viii-ix

Nuts, 147, 148


Oils, xi

Onions, 20

Orange and Chile Sauce, 54, 67

Orange-Flavored Chicken, 114-115

Orange-Rice Pudding, 144

Oranges and orange flavoring, 54, 67,
114-115, 144, 145, 146


Papaya nectar, 49

Parsley, 61

Pasilla chiles, 23

Pasta, 134-135, 138-139, 141

Pecan and Pine Nut Dessert, 147

Pecans, 147, 148

Pequito Tunas Triangles, 12

Pesto, 47

Pine nuts, 147

Pinto Bean Frijoles, 70

Pinto beans, 33, 65, 70

Pisto Manchego-Style Stewed
Peppers and Squash, 71

Poblano chiles, 6

Pollo Escabache, 112

Pollo Escondido, 56, 113

Pollo Naranja, 114-115

Pork, 72-73, 89, 116-117, 118-119.
See also Ham

Pork and Black Bean Burritos, 72-73

Pork Tamales, 118-119

Pork-Stuffed Brandied Turkey
Medallions, 116-117

Potato Salad Southwestern Style, 21

Potato Skins with Chile Poblano, 6-7

Potatoes, 6-7, 21, 68, 77

Pudding, 144, 146

Puerto Penasco Spicy Fish Tacos, 74-75


Quail Breasts with Cilantro Salsa, 120

Queso anejo, 136


Radishes, 4

Red Chile Sauce–Enchilada Style,
55, 72, 73, 78, 96

Red chili, 34-36

Reynaldo's Spiced Sweet Carrots, 69

Rice, 64, 76, 80, 85, 144

❖

Rice pudding, 144

Romaine lettuce, 16, 18, 20, 22

Romaine-Spinach Salad with
    Watercress Dressing, 22

Ruidoso Rainbows, 8-9


Salad dressings, 20, 22, 45, 61

Salmon, 23

Salsa Basil, 56, 113, 136

Salsa Basil con Pasta, 56, 136

Salsa Flamenco, 57

Salsa Fresca, 10

Salsa Mole, 58-59, 104, 110-111

Salsa Tequila, 60, 104-105

Salsas, 10, 46, 56, 57, 58-59, 60

Salt substitute, x, xi

Sea bass, 11, 121

Sea Bass Flamenco, 121

Seviche Matamoros, 11

Shrimp, 138-139

Sirloin Tip Fajitas, 122

Smoked Salmon and Pasilla Chile Salad, 23

Socorro Caldillo, 37

Sodium, viii-ix, xi

Sofia's Chile Jelly Buñuelos, 148

Sonoran Green Rice, 76

Sopaipillas, 140, 148

Sour Cream-Parsley Dressing, 20, 61

Spanish Rice, 64

Spanish Trail Twice-Baked Spuds, 77

Spices
   mail-order sources, 151

Spicy Beef Tacos, 78

Spicy Triple Noodle Casserole, 141

Spinach, 22

Squash, 33, 71

Strawberries Vegas, 145

Strawberry-Vanilla Sauce, 150

Sweet and sour zucchini, 79


Tacos, 74-75, 78

Tamales, 118-119

Tequila, 8, 9, 48, 60

Texican Sweet and Sour Zucchini, 79

Tomato Bisque, 30-31

Tomato Chile Gravy, 40, 92-93

Tomatoes, 10, 30-31, 32, 40

Tortillas, 8-9, 67, 78

Trout, 124-125

Truchas Nuevo Mexico, 124-125

Tuna, 12

Turbinado sugar, xii

Turkey, 14, 116-117


Venison Caliente, 126-127

Vinegar, 44


Watercress Dressing, 22

Whistlin' Dixie Creole Rice and
    Red Beans, 80

Wild Turkey Jerky, 14

Wine, 82, 85, 90, 100, 112, 114, 118, 1138


Yogurt, 146,


Zucchini, 24, 79

# About the Author

❖

BOB WISEMAN has had a serious interest in the cooking of the greater Southwest since he moved to Las Vegas, Nevada, in 1954. A lifetime member of the International Chili Society, Bob met his wife, Jodi, at a chile cook off in Boulder City, Nevada, in 1986, and married her at another in Ajijic, Jalisco, Mexico, in 1989. Each year Bob and Jodi compete in chili contests in Mexico, Hawaii, and most western states. Their walls are decorated with plaques and trophies documenting their success.

Bob has taught cooking classes featuring the food styles of China, India, Spain, and the Southwest. In 1981, he attended an eighteen-month culinary course at Caesar's Palace in Las Vegas, where he learned cooking techniques of France, Spain, China, Japan, India, Latin America, Home-spun America, and others. The class was featured on many television and radio programs, including the Merv Griffin show.

In addition to publishing more than one hundred recipes in various journals, magazines, and newspapers, Bob has written three not-yet-published novels and has seen into print many pieces of short fiction and articles on western history and travel. He is proud to be an active member of the Western Writers of America.

# About the Photographer

❖

OWEN LOWE graduated from the
Art Institute of Philadelphia in 1984
and returned to his native Arizona
three years later. He now lives in
Flagstaff, where he specializes in
medium-and large-format studio
and location photography for adver-
tising, corporate/industrial and
scenic assignments.

# SHARE THE SOUTHWEST WITH A FRIEND

*Use this convenient form to order additional copies of* Healthy Southwestern Cooking *as well as these other fine cookbooks:*

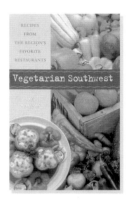

*by* JUDY WALKER *and* KIM MACEACHERN

Seventy-five easy ways to make salsa with spunk, dip with zing, and chips with lots of pizzazz. *72 pages, 28 color photographs, 8 x 8 softcover, \$9.95*

*by* RITA DAVENPORT *art by* TED DE GRAZIA

De Grazia's whimsical renderings of the Southwest along with Rita Davenport's classic recipes make this a useful and attractive guide to south-of-the-border cooking. *88 pages, 83 pages of illustrations, 6 x 9 softcover, \$12.95*

*by* JUDY WALKER

Southwestern recipes that have been simplified from their more traditional versions, without sacrificing the rich variety of flavors. *144 pages, 30 color illustrations, 6 x 9 softcover, \$14.95*

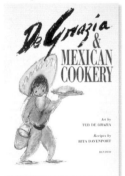

*by* JUDY WALKER *and* KIM MACEACHERN

Perfect for the cook-on-the-go, these one-hundred recipes of Southwestern soups, stews, and skillet suppers are easy to prepare and make clean up a snap. *128 pages, 13 color photos, 8 x 8 softcover, \$12.95*

*by* LON WALTERS

Flavorful and colorful vegetarian combinations from the region's favorite restaurants unlock the incredible flavors of the Southwest. *176 pages, 15 color photographs, 6 x 9 softcover, \$14.95*